Prospecting

For Gold in

California

Panning, Dredging and Metal Detection on Public Access Sites

Alton Pryor

Stagecoach Publishing
5360 Campcreek Loop
Roseville, California 95747
916-771-8166
stagecoach@surewest.net

Prospecting For Gold in California

Panning, Dredging and Metal Detection on Public Access Sites

ISBN: 978-0-692-43809-1
Library of Congress Control No.: 2015906686

Alton Pryor

Stagecoach Publishing
5360 Campcreek Loop
Roseville, California 95747
916-771-8166
stagecoach@surewest.net

More gold has been mined from the thoughts of man than has been taken from the earth.—Napoleon Hill

Table of Contents

Introduction

We have had numerous requests from readers to publish a book on public access sites that allow gold panning, dredging and metal detecting. At first, we ignored the requests, thinking the number wanting such access were at a minimum.

As the years have gone on and the requests for such information have increased, we've changed our mind. "Maybe there is a need for such a book," we've told our self.

We hope that this publication helps to fill the void for such information.

Chapter 1

Panning for Gold

Since the days of the California Gold Rush, people have lusted for their chance to find gold. Gold is still out there for those hardy enough to seek it.

It's said that 95 percent of the gold in California has never been found. A caveat to that statement, however, is that much of the gold remaining in California is difficult if not impossible to access.

Still, there is a thrill to finding that gold nugget, and people still flock to areas where recreational gold panning is allowed.

A simple gold pan is used to separate sand and gravel From gold flakes.

A simple gold pan is effective in detecting and recovering gold from a streambed. Recreational gold panning is a popular hobby that can provide a lot of fun and hopefully profit for a family.

Today, there are inexpensive and lightweight sluice boxes that can help the beginner separate his gold from the gravel of the moving stream. Metal detectors can be valuable tools for the gold seeker.

A typical dry washer for arid areas.

Dry washers can be used in areas where water is not available, such as arid and desert areas. Dry washing goes back to the earliest days of gold discovery, where water was not available to separate the minerals from waste sand and rock.

Miners devised crude methods of utilizing the flow of air and vibration to concentrate and separate valuable materials like gold and gemstones from waste material.

Gold mining, prospecting and panning locations in California extend from the Mexican border to the Oregon state line. Gold is found in California's adjoining states of Nevada and Arizona as well.

Chapter 2

Gold Prospecting Maps

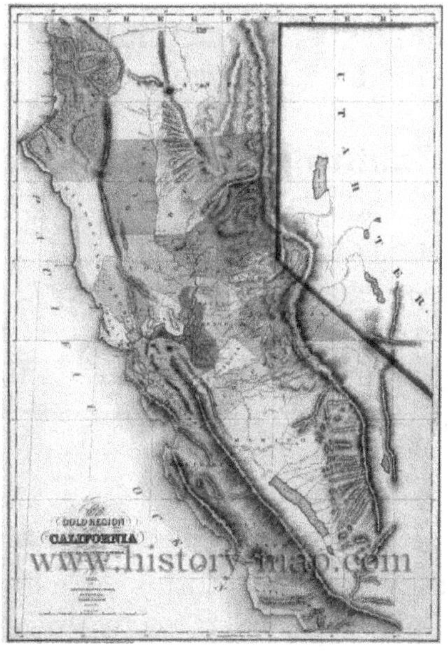

California Gold Map

California provides invaluable resources for the gold seeker in the form of "California gold maps". In these maps are lists of towns near which gold deposits exist.

A set of six California gold maps is available showing regions 1 through 6.

California Gold Region 1

Map Number 1 shows 405 gold mines and prospecting sites adjacent to Arizona and Nevada from Mexico to Death Valley. Shown on this map are Yuma, the Colorado River, Picacho, Pot Holes, Glamis, Brawley, Salton Sea, Blythe and Needles.

This area is of especial interest for treasure hunters having metal detectors.

California Gold Region 2

This document lists 340 gold mines and prospecting sites in Gold Region 2. This region includes San Diego, Escondido, Santa Ana, Riverside, Palm Springs, Indio, Julian, Banner, Dulzura, Jacumba, and El Centro.

There are gold mines, prospecting and panning sites in the mountains, streams and national forests. Excellent camping, fishing, hiking and recreational vehicle facilities can be found in California Gold Region 2.

California Gold Region 3

There are 513 gold mines, prospecting and panning sites listed on Gold Region 3 map.

This region includes Los Angeles, Ventura, San Bernardino, Big Bear Lake, Lancaster, Palmdale, Barstow, Victorville and Twenty Nine Palms. There are also some prospecting sites in San Gabriel, Tehachapi and the San Bernardino Mountains. Frazier Mountain and Piru Creek gold deposits can be found on this map.

California Gold Region 4

In Gold Region 4, there are 770 gold mines and prospecting sites listed. This region includes such well-known mining towns as Randsburg, Johannesburg and Trona.

Included are Mojave, China Lake, Bakersfield, Porterville, Fresno, Fort Irwin, and the Sierra, Sequoia and Inyo National Forests.

This region 4 map shows the Kings, Kern and Owens rivers, and the Slate, El Paso and Inyo Mountains.

Treasure hunters with metal detectors like to “gold nugget shoot” in this gold prospecting and mining region. Prospectors like panning for gold in these streams as well.

California Gold Region 5

This region has the greatest number of gold mines and prospecting sites of any of California’s gold regions, with 3,000 gold mines listed.

The region extends from about 40 miles south of Yosemite National Park to Quincy and Paradise in the north, and eastward from Sacramento to Lake Tahoe.

Included in this region are the cities of Jamestown, Columbia, Grass Valley, Downieville, Merced, Mariposa and Marysville, as well as eight national forests.

Here will be found the "Ancient (Tertiary) Rivers of Gold" (see Chapter 3), as well as the American, Calaveras, Cosumnes, Feather, Merced, Mokelumne, Sacramento, Stanislaus, Tuolumne and Yuba gold-bearing rivers.

Gold Region 5 is considered a world class gold prospecting and gold panning region.

California Gold Region 6

Gold mines, prospecting and panning extend from the north edge of Map 5 to the Oregon state line. There are 1,580 gold mines and prospecting locations listed.

The Klamath, Trinity and Smith rivers are good gold panning sites. The towns of Redding, Shasta, Susanville, Whiskeytown, French Gulch, Weed, Alturas, Orleans, Happy Camp and Crescent City are listed on the Region 6 map.

Gold production in this region was second only to that of the California Mother Lode.

Chapter 3

Ancient Rivers of Gold

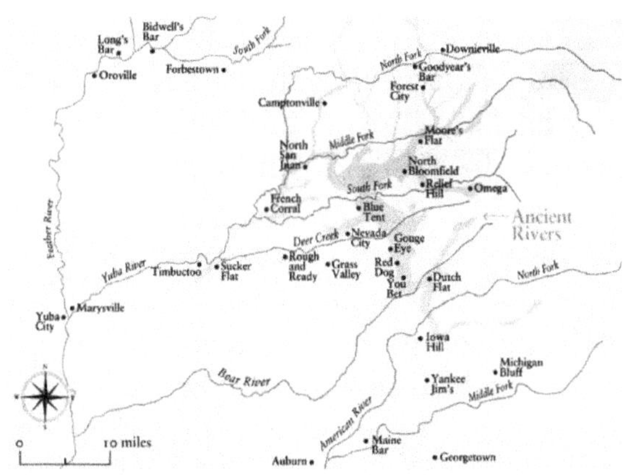

Map of Ancient Rivers of Gold

The Ancient Rivers of Gold existed during the Tertiary Period. The Tertiary Period occurred from 66 million to 2.58 million years ago.

Even then, many of them had large quantities of gold in their gravels. Because of that, they are known as the "Ancient Rivers of Gold." The Tertiary period is the age when mammals began.

The now-dry Tertiary rivers are thought to be a prime source of the gold found in many of the rivers and streams in Northern California. Historic information on these rivers is based on the work of

Waldemar Lindgren, United States Geological Survey.

The paths of these ancient rivers are often interrupted and follow tortuous routes. The rivers have been altered by volcanic activity, erosion, and in some instances, the rivers have been covered with lava.

Volcanic flows have been found up to 4,000 feet deep and 60 miles in length. Portions of an ancient river may be found at ground level, near the top of a mountain, on the side of a mountain, or even buried.

Early prospectors found portions of the ancient rivers and worked them for their rich gold content. Later, mining companies used hydraulic mining or drift mining techniques to recover the gold.

Drift mining is used to access a variety of minerals such as gold, coal, quartz and zinc. Drift mining involves the drilling of a horizontal tunnel below the volcanic covering to reach the mineral seams.

The gold or other mineral deposits are extracted by underground mining methods and then washed at the mouth of the tunnel. The tunnels can also be used for ventilation and exploration of other mineral deposits.

Geologic reports note gravel deposits up to 250 feet deep with gold deposits intersperse at various levels without the gravels. In some areas, the gravels of these ancient streams have been cemented together. Smaller materials between the larger gravels have bound the larger gravels together.

Many miles of these ancient rivers are still unworked and believed to be very rich in gold.

Diamond deposits have been found along with the gold at Cherokee Flat in Butte County and in the gravels at Placerville, in El Dorado County.

The diamonds that have been found are gerally of small size and yellowish in color.

Yuba Ancient River of Gold

The Yuba Ancient River of Gold is the largest of the Tertiary rivers of the Sierra Nevada. This river runs through or into the counties of Plumas, Sierra, Yuba, Nevada, Placer and El Dorado.

Ancient Yuba has branches wandering throughout the area between Marysville and Lake Tahoe. The famous gold towns of Grass Valley and Nevada City are along the course of the Ancient Yuba, as are the gold deposit sites south of Downieville in the Tahoe National Forest.

The deepest trough-shaped depressions in the drainage basin of the Tertiary Yuba River are filled to a depth of 50 to 200 feet by course gravels that that have been cemented so they can't be washed without crushing.

American Ancient River of Gold

The Tertiary American River follows a more or less east to west course from south of Lake Tahoe to the town of Roseville northeast of Sacramento. It crosses Highway 49 a couple of miles south of Placerville, a gold-rich community in California.

Ancient Intervolcanic American River

The Ancient Intervolcanic American River of Gold has many gold deposit sites along its course. It starts in Tahoe National Forest near the North Fork of the present-day American River.

The ancient stream then winds its way southwesterly to Auburn in Placer County. One branch of the Ancient Intervolcanic American River circles around Volcanoville, which is noted for its gold bearing gravels.

Ancient Magalia Channel

Magalia Channel is just north of Paradise in Butte County. There are gold sites on both sides of the channel. A 54-pound nugget was found at Magalia.

The west branch of the Feather River runs near and crosses this ancient channel south of Last Chance Creek.

Ancient Jura River

The Ancient Jura River is from the Jurassic Period, which makes it older than the ancient rivers of the Tertiary Period.

The course of this ancient river traces from Sierra County past Blairsden and Cromberg in Plumas County and Mount Ingalls. Very few gold sites are located along the Jura River.

Mokelumne Ancient River of Gold

The Mokelumne Ancient River of Gold starts in El Dorado National Forest and runs westward. It terminates about eight miles west of California State Highway 49 not far from the town of Plymouth in Amador County.

Two branches of the river originate near the North Fork of the Cosumnes River. Quite a few gold sites are said to lie along the westernmost branch and along the main course of the ancient river near the towns of Volcano and Plymouth.

Calaveras Ancient River of Gold

This stream parallels the South Fork of the Stanislaus River just north of Columbus Historical State Park. There are numerous gold sites along the Tertiary Ancient Calaveras River of Gold.

The river continues westward to California State Highway 49 and parallels the gold camps north to San Andreas. It terminates near Valley Springs in Calaveras County.

Tuolumne Ancient River of Gold

Paralleling the present-day Tuolumne River, the Tertiary Tuolumne River starts at Oakland Recreation Camp in the Stanislaus National Forest and runs to Chinese Camp by Highway 49.

Gold sites are located both north and south of this ancient river and nears the towns of Coulterville, Jacksonville, Jamestown and Tuolumne.

Ancient Intervolcanic Cataract Channel

The Ancient Intervolcanic Cataract Channel originates in Calaveras Big Trees National Forest in Tuolumne County.

It crosses the north fork of the Stanislaus River into Calaveras County. It then crosses the Stanislaus River near Carson Hill, Columbia State Park and Squabbletown.

The channel continues southwesterly a few miles west of Senora and Jamestown and terminates at the Tuolumne/Stanislaus County line.

Gold deposits exist at each of the towns mentioned.

Chapter 4

Public Access Sites

The Bureau of Land Management is the agency that administers federal land. Much of the public land administered by BLM is open for filing of mining claims under the Mining Law of 1872.

The law is under heavy scrutiny by environmental organizations such as Earthworks, headquartered in Washington, D.C.

Earthworks calls the Mining Law of 1872 "One of the last remaining dinosaurs of the old west."

While critics of the law are trying to change the present system, mining companies are putting up strong resistance. The bitter battle over the Mining Law of 1872 has gone on for years and is likely to go on for many more years.

Critics argue that a law passed in 1872 is due for an overhaul. Among the criticisms of the law is the absence of royalties paid to the government. The criticism is whether the public is receiving "a fair return" for the use of public land.

On the other hand, the changes being proposed by the critics would bring about a major decline in domestic mining and would do little to improve environmental protection.

Cartoon in 1861 shows prospector defending his mining claim.

The Mining Law of 1872 emerged as a product of the California Gold Rush and other western mining booms of the mid-19th century. The law gave wide discretion over the use of public land resources to the private sector.

Little public administration was required, allowing miners to implement their own customs, codes and laws. The central provisions of this law remain intact today.

Free access is a cornerstone of the Mining Law. If a site contains a deposit that can be profitably marketed, claimants enjoy the "right to mine", regardless of any alternative use.

Miners organized their own governments in each new mining camp. For example, in Rough and

Ready in Nevada County, miners adopted the Mexican mining laws then existing in California.

The little gold camp of Rough and Ready once attempted to secede from the U.S. While the attempt was unsuccessful, the community still holds its annual secession celebration, which is more of a beer bust than a celebration.

Western representatives successfully argued that western miners and prospectors were performing a public service by promoting commerce and settling new territory.

In 1865, Congress passed a law that instructed courts deciding mining rights issues to ignore federal ownership and defer to the miners in actual possession of the ground.

Eastern legislators didn't always agree with their Western counterparts. One proposal introduced advocated sending armed forces to California, Colorado and Arizona to expel miners from their claims.

The legislator suggested the federal government work the mines for the benefit of the treasury.

In 1872, Congress amended the mining law to limit the size of a claim. A maximum size of lode claims was 1500 feet long and 600 feet wide. The new law also set the price of a mining claim to range from $2.50 per acre to $5.00 per acre. This price has remained the same since 1872.

Persons wishing to file a mining claim in California should contact the Bureau of Land Management in Sacramento.

In other states, the same advice applies; contact the BLM in the state's capital or field offices.

There are a number of public access sites for people wanting to try their hand at gold prospecting. Listed in alphabetical order are some in California.

Butte Recreation Area

This site lies 25 miles Northeast of Chico in northern California. The forks of Butte Recreation area have trails through steep pine and fir covered canyons.

Panning and sluicing permits are available by contacting BLM in the Redding Field Office. There are multiple mineral collection sites to reserve along the creek.

Trails in the area follow steep canyon walls with a mixed vegetation of Ponderosa Pine, Douglas Fir and Madrone.

Discharge of firearms is prohibited in the Recreation area except for shooting legal game during the hunting season.

Permits are required for low-impact gold panning and sluicing in the Forks of Butte Creek Recreation Area. There are 26 sites that can be reserved for $5 per day for up to 30 days per years.

Permits are issued from May through October, depending on road and weather conditions.

To obtain a mineral collection permit, call the BLM Field Office in Redding: (530) 224-2100. The office can then email, fax or mail you an application packet.

Keyesville Recreation Area

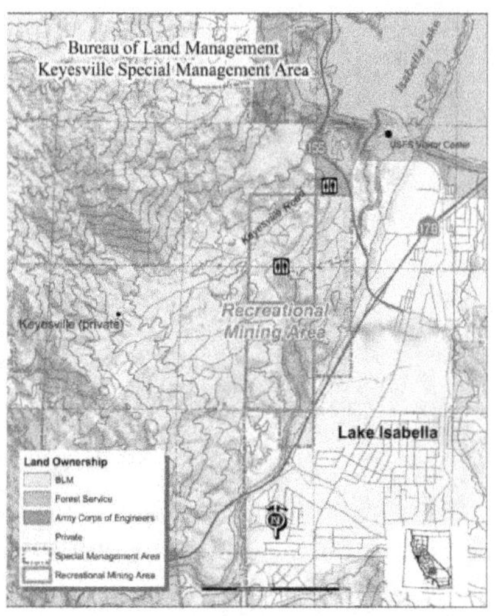

Map of Keyesville Special Recreation Management Area.

"Advertencia! El Rio Kern es muy peligroso!"

This Spanish language message is used to announce the dangerous river waters in the Keyesville Recreation Area. This area, located near the communities of Lake Isabella and Kernville, consists of approximately 7,000 acres of BLM managed land.

Bunkhouse at Mammoth Consolidate Mine.

The area offers a wide range of recreational activities, including white-water rafting, biking, gold prospecting and hunting and fishing.

In 1851 gold was discovered on Greenhorn Creek near the Kern River by an exploration party sent out by John C. Fremont. This led to the first Kern River Gold Rush.

A stampede of miners rushed to the area in 1854 when placer gold was found in the Kern River. Even before this discovery, Richard Keys found lode gold in 1852.

The town of Petersburgh, near the summit of Greenhorn Mountain, was established about 1858 and became an important supply point. The earthen Keyesville Fort was built during the Tule River Indian War of 1856 to protect settlers. The fort was never utilized.

High above Old Mammoth, California is the site of Mammoth Consolidated Mine, which was founded around circa 1927-1933.

In 1927, A.G. Mahan, Sr., his son, Arch, and several partners, purchased the claims under the name of Mammoth Consolidated Mining Company. Early samples indicated six-tenths of an ounce of gold and one-fifth of an ounce of silver per ton or rock.

At 1927 prices, this amounted to $12.70 per ton. Iron sulfides made extraction of the valuable metals very expensive. About $100,000 worth of gold was pulled out of the mine. Some doubt that it paid the expenses for its extraction.

A miner made $5.25 per day which was considered good pay. From that amount, $1.25 per day was deducted for the miner's room and board.

Much of the ore processing mill still remains.

The Keysville Recreation area receives a high amount of recreational use because of its access to the Lower Kern River and the availability of trails to off-highway vehicles and mountain bikes.

The Keyesville area played a significant role in the expansion of the American West. Joseph R. Walker led one of John C. Fremont's expeditions over Walker Pass in1834, giving him the honor of being the first white man to enter Kern Valley.

Today, the historic town site of Keyesville is located on private land and is little more than a ghost town.

Redding Resource Area

No permit is required for low-impact gold panning in this area except at the Forks of Butte Creek Recreation Area.

Popular areas for panning are along Clear Creek and the Trinity River.

There is a moratorium on the issue of dredging permits in the state of California.

This area offers many opportunities for hiking, biking and horseback riding on the network of non-motorized trails surrounding the Redding area.

Chapter 5

Gold Around the State

Alameda County

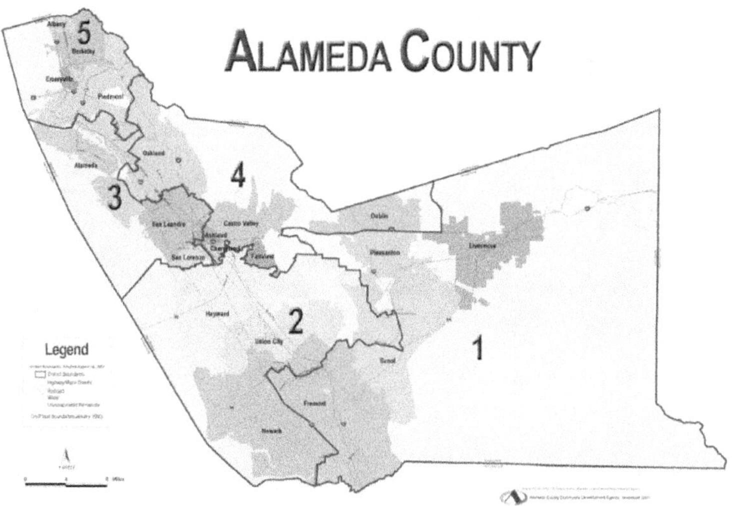

Map of Alameda County

About the only incident of gold in Alameda County involves George Patterson, who, with his two brothers, built a home in 1857. He called it Ardenwood, after the forested area in England that is mentioned in Shakespeare's play, "As You Like It."

According to George's son Donald, his father buried 40 to 50 slugs of gold in his backyard. Many members of the family have tried to locate the buried treasure but it has never been found.

Money was found stashed in the door frames of the house. Some of the rooms have secret entrances and exits.

Before the European settlement of the San Francisco Bay, the Ohlone tribe of Indians occupied the area. Spanish settlement occurred in the 18th century when Juan Bautista de Anza led an expedition to the area.

Alpine County

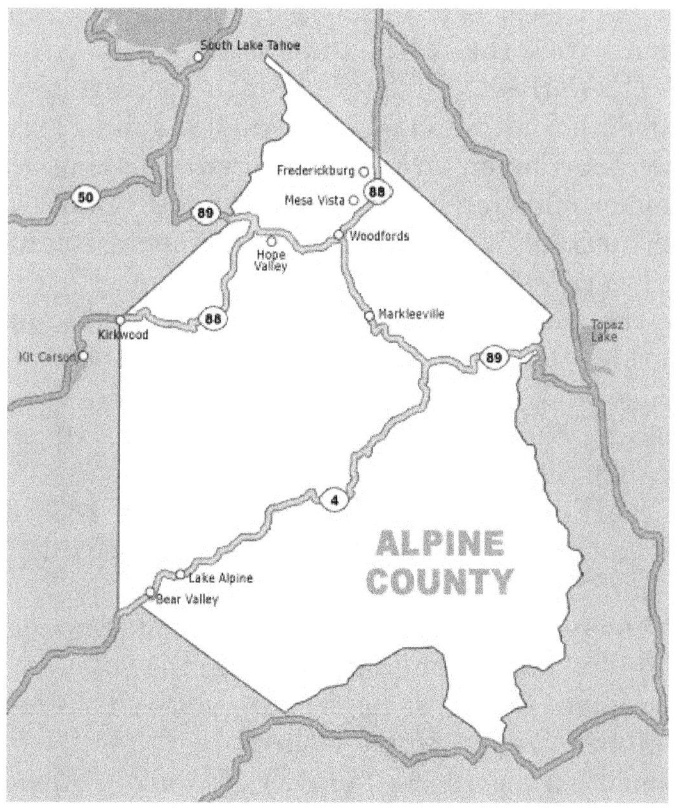

Map of Alpine County

It was silver, not gold that brought settlement to Alpine County. Following the discovery of the Comstock Lode near Virginia City, Nevada, in 1859, thousands of prospectors swarmed into the eastern Nevada looking for riches.

A year earlier, a group of Scandinavians found rich silver outcrops near Silver Creek and established the town of Silver Mountain.

The first people to settle in what is now Alpine County were the Washo Indians.

The earliest explorers through the region were Jedediah Smith and Joseph Walker. John Fremont and Kit Carson are credited with making their famous midwinter trip across Alpine County and the Sierra Nevada in 1844 that brought attention to the travel routes across the mountain.

The silver boom was short-lived. In 1861, Jacob Markley took out a 160-acre claim and built a bridge and toll station on the banks of a stream crossing the road from Genoa, Nevada, 10 miles south of Silver City.

Markley was killed in a gunfight in 1863, but his name was given to the town of Markleeville, the County Seat of Alpine County.

Today, Alpine County holds the distinction of being the least populated county in the state.

Alpine County's name was derived from its similarity to the alpine country of Europe. It was formed from parts of El Dorado, Amador, Calaveras, Tuolumne and Mono counties.

The spark to creating Alpine County came from the discovery of silver ore in several locations in the late 1850s and early 1860s.

For best gold mining sites, go to the Bureau of Land Management Office for the area and purchase one or the entire set of their site maps.

Amador County

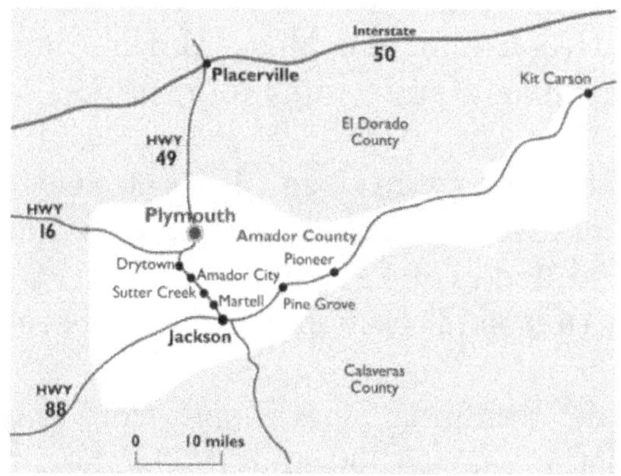

Map of Amador County

Amador County has been one of the most productive gold producing areas in the Mother Lode. Amador County produced 6,500,000 ounces of placer gold and 7,700,000 ounces of lode gold.

Placer is pronounced plas-er, not pley-ser. It is a word derived from Spanish referring to an alluvial or eluvial deposit of gravel containing particles of valuable minerals such as gold, silver or platinum.

A "lode" is a mineral deposit consisting of a zone of veins in solid rock. Most prospectors think of lodes as veins. This is partially correct but a vein is only one type of lode.

Gold is heavy, roughly 19 times heavier than water. Consequently, gold particles of any substantive size do not tend to move far from the source.

Placer gold tends to move downward, sinking as deep as it can following the path of least resistance.

Amador County was formed in 1854 and named after native Californian Jose Maria Amador. The first gold quartz mine in California was started at Amador City.

Jackson, the county seat, has the deepest mines on the Continent, which produced more than half of the gold mined in the Mother Lode.

With that said, let's move on to where the gold really is.

Sizable dredging operations were carried on between the years 1850 and 1950. The Big Indian Creek area produced 100,000 ounces of placer gold near Fiddletown along Indian Gulch, which runs into Big Indian Creek. Big Indian Creek is said to contain placer gold in large quantities. The Plymouth area of Amador County is said to be rich in placer gold.

Amador City

Amador City is the smallest incorporated city in California (some say in the United State). One of the most productive mines, the Keystone Mine, is located at Amador City.

Amador City's street names paint a unique picture and bring a chuckle to newcomers. Among them are: God's Hill, Cross Street, Pig Turd Alley, Church Street, Bunker Hill, Water Street and Stringbean Alley.

Amador City Hotel is the oldest structure in town and was built around 1855.

Amador City offers a free guided walking tour that takes about an hour to complete.

Some historians believe 4,000 people lived in Amador City during the Gold Rush. Today it is a prime example of a historic town retaining its look and feel of a surviving Gold Rush town.

Drytown

Somebody was drinking and in their cups when they named this community. At one time, Drytown had 26 saloons.

It really got its name from Dry Creek, which runs dry during the summer. It was also the focal point for the prohibition movement in California.

A blacksmith shop with marble floors is the oldest building in Amador County.

A fire destroyed most of the town in 1857. Most of Dry Town's inhabitants packed up and moved to more successful mines.

The town was saved by the construction of Highway 49 through the town in 1920.

Fiddletown

Fiddletown was settled by Missourians in 1849. In the 1850s, it served as a trading center for mining camps.

Fiddletown had one of the largest Chinese populations in California. According to an 1860 census, more than 2,000 Chinese lived in Fiddletown.

Placer mining was the most popular mining technique. This presented a problem for Fiddletown miners as the local water source was Dry Creek, which ran dry during the summer months.

Fiddletown lacked the deep quartz mines which would have sustained it when the placers played out. When the gold was gone, so were the residents.

The town got a name change in 1878. One resident, Judge Columbus Allen Purinton, of Fiddletown, lobbied the legislature to have the town's name changed.

He asked that it be changed to "Oleta", which just incidentally was the name of his daughter.

The Chew Kee store was a rammed earth building and one of the few such structures left in the Mother Lode.

Judge Purinton was never a judge in Amador County, but was well-known in Sacramento and San Francisco. He claimed he was embarrassed to write "Fiddletown" as his place of residence.

The legislature approved Purinton's request. But in 1932, during the eighty-third anniversary celebration of the founding of Fiddletown, residents began to wonder why was the name changed?

Once again, it was decided to change the name again, this time from "Oleta" back to "Fiddletown". This change did not require an act of the legislature.

All the residents had to do was get at least sixty four residents to sign a petition, send it to the U.S.

Postal Department and the Postmaster General. In early June, 1932, the news came through that Fiddletown was once more its old self, a genuine Gold Rush treasure. The poor town of "Oleta" simply died.

Jackson

The town of Jackson was originally named "Bottileas" by Mexican and Chilean miners. They were impressed with the number of bottles dropped at a spring that served as a watering hole for passing miners.

It was given its final name after Alden Appola Moore Jackson, a local lawyer who was liked by the gold miners.

A little skullduggery was involved in choosing a county seat for Amador County and involved the county seat of Calaveras County as well as Amador. In 1851, both Jackson and Mokelumne Hill vied for the county seat.

When Calaveras County was organized, Double Springs obtained the County Seat. Double Springs had but one house, which answered as Court House, saloon, store and hotel. The area was really reaching out for a more suitable County Seat.

Jackson was quite willing to accommodate. Since elections and Acts of the legislature involved too much time, a plan was enacted.

Charles Boynton and Theo Mudge walked up to the County Seat's bar, threw down a coin and invited all hands to imbibe. Residents readily agreed to the invitation.

Among the celebrants was Colonel Collyer, the County Clerk, who also loved good whiskey. While most of the town's residents were getting sloshed, another detachment gathered the county seat archives and hauled them away to Jackson.

Colonel Collyer was naturally abashed to find the County Seat of Double Springs had disappeared and moved to Jackson. He swore the army should be called out to vindicate the dignity of the court.

Jackson became the county seat of the newly formed Amador County in 1854. In a vote for the location of the county seat in the May 1851 election, 1,224 votes were cast for Moquelumne Hill and 1,014 votes for Jackson.

An armed party from Moquelumne Hill pursued Judge William Fowler Smith, who proclaimed Jackson as the winner of the county seat.

Plymouth

There is very little in Plymouth to remind you of the Gold Rush days.

The head frame and tailings from the Plymouth Consolidated Mines are still evident. The mine did produce $13 million in gold.

Now Plymouth survives as an agro-center with an emphasis on the Shenandoah Valley vineyards to the east of town.

The historic D' Agostini Winery is eight miles east of town and it's possible to walk through its original wine cellar with its hand-hewn beams, old oak casks, and walls of solid rock quarried from nearby hills.

Leland Stanford made a bundle in Sutter Creek, owning shares in the Lincoln Mine. Once he tried to sell his interest in the mine for $5,000 but couldn't find a buyer. He later sold it for $400,000.

Plymouth was settled in 1871 by Green Aden and others in search of quartz. The town grew because of the potential for quartz mining.

Hetty Green

The town took a sudden jump in population when the mines were purchased by Hayward, D.O. Mills and Company in 1873.

The only hydraulic powered foundry in the United States is still in operation here, powered by a 42-inch water wheel. Visitors are welcome.

Hetty Green, once considered the richest woman in the world (nick-named the "Witch of Wall Street"), was the owner of the Old Eureka Mine.

Sutter Gold Mining Incorporated entered into a lease agreement to acquire 132 acres of land adjacent to the company's properties in Plymouth. The purchase was identified as the Old Eureka and the Central Eureka

The Central Eureka originally opened as the Summit Mine in 1855. After being idle after 1875, it was purchased for $6,000 by the Central Eureka Mining Company.

The mine then operated profitably until 1942, when the Federal Government's War Production Board Order L-208 suspended all gold mining operations. The mine reopened in 1946 and operated until 1958.

Plymouth is the gateway to the Shenandoah Valley which has 21 wineries. Daffodil Hill, hiking, gold panning, wine tasting, and boating are all diversions available around the Plymouth area.

Butte County

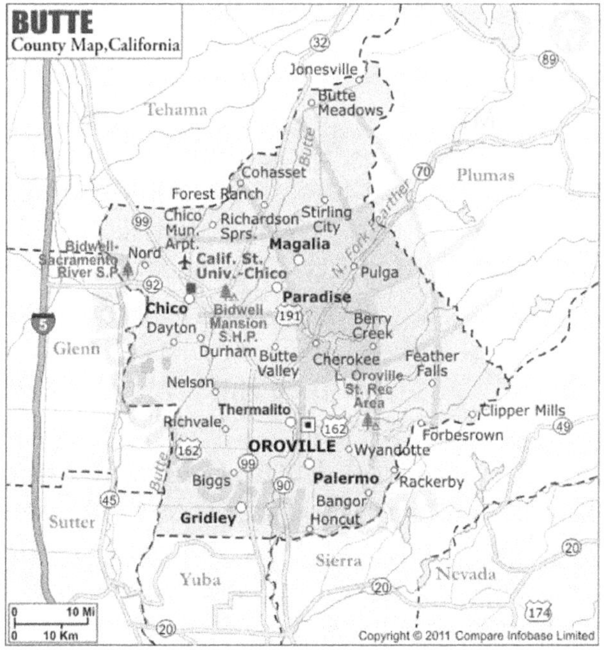

Butte County Map

Butte County has maintained a high position among the gold-producing counties of California. Very little has been published on the geology and production of its mining districts.

Magalia

This region was extensively mined during and after the gold rush. A 54-pound nugget was found here in 1859.

Estimates have put the gold output of this area at $40 million, but that figure is considered high. Much of the output has come from drift mines.

Oroville

Gravels from the flood plain of the Feather River yielded 1,964,130 ounces of gold from1903 to 1959. This made the Oroville district the largest producer in Butte County.

Yankee Hill

Located in central Butte County, most of the lode production from the county occurred here.

From 1929 through 1959, the district produced 34,427 ounces of gold from lode mines and 5,154 ounces from placer mines.

Production before 1910 was about $1,520,000 (57,000 ounces), mostly from the Hearst Mine.

Calaveras County

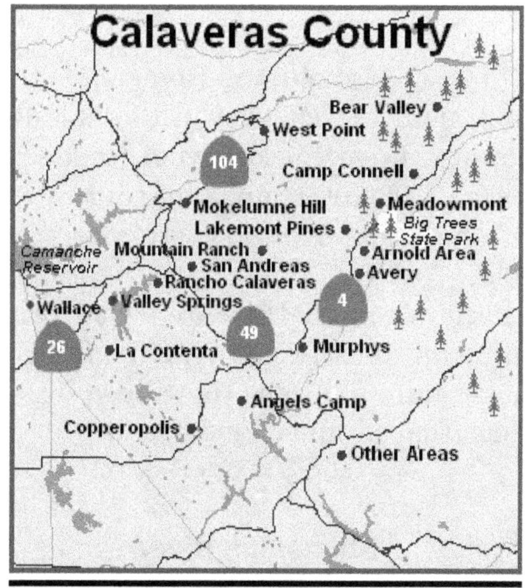

Calaveras County Map

After placer gold was discovered in 1849, rich lode veins were opened in 1850 above the placer workings. Placer gold production is estimated at 2,415,000 ounces and lode gold at 2,045,700 ounces.

Calaveras River

The Calaveras River channel and all tributaries contain rich placer deposits. In the Table Mountain area placers were very rich in gold ore.

In the Jenny Lind district, large scale dredge and dragline operations took place with an estimated 1,000,000 ounces of gold being recovered.

Mokelumne River

In the Comanche District in the northwest part of the county, huge bucket-type dredge recovered an estimated 1,000,000 ounces of gold.

All of the area tributary streams are rich in placer gold.

The Pern Mine in this area was originally a copper mine but had a rich by-product of gold.

At Mokelumne Hill are the Elipse, Infernal and other mines that produced lode gold.

Stanislaus River

Angels Camp had many area mines, including the Keystone, Lancha Plana, and Union mines. The Utica and Union mines were major producers of lode gold.

The Melones district contained more than 800 lode mines. Carson Hill was considered the most productive with rich lode deposits.

The Sheep Ranch Mine and the Royal Mine both produced a lot of lode gold.

Colusa County

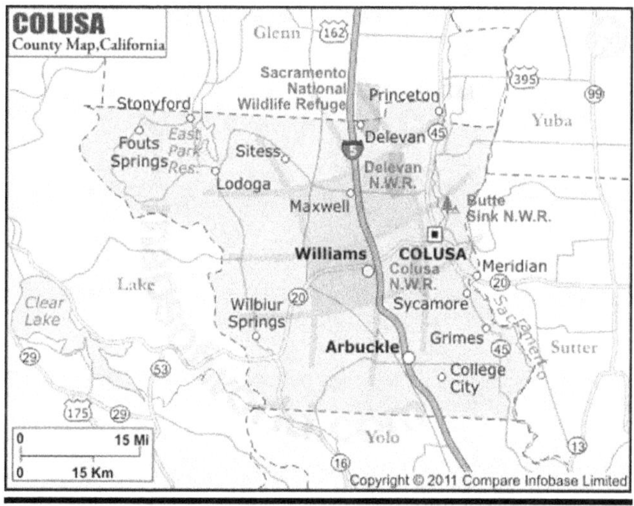

Colusa County Map

Colusa County was named for a Mexican land grant held by John Bidwell. The grant was called *Rancho Colus* after an Indian tribe on the west side of the Sacramento River.

The Sulphur Creek mercury-gold district is in the southwest corner of Colusa County. Gold was discovered there in 1865.

The principal source has been the Manzanita Mine. Gold has also been found at the Cherry Hill and Clyde Mines.

Contra Costa County

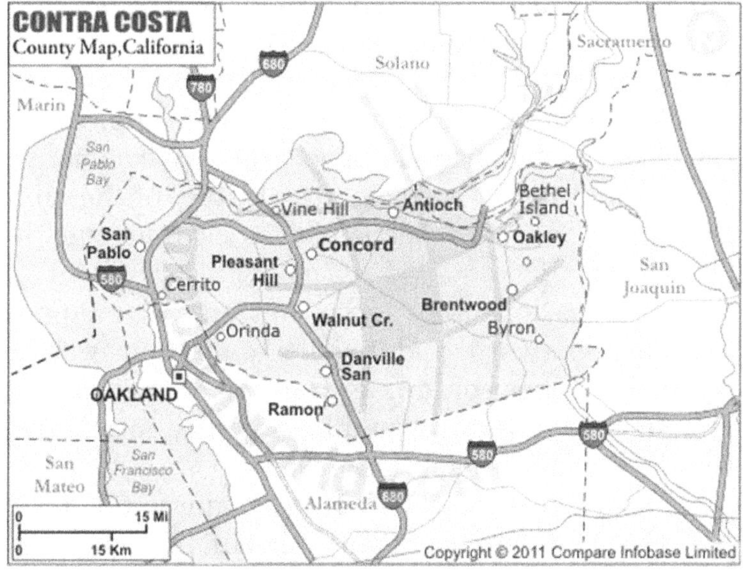

Map of Contra Costa County

In his retirement years, Jack Wessman adopted an unusual hobby. He used heavy equipment in an effort to clean up old mercury mine on Mount Diablo.

Wessman purchased 109-acre property on Mount Diablo in 1974. He knew there was an old mine there but didn't anticipate the expense and headache that came with it.

He battled regulators on one hand and with the other, contoured drainages, capped waste rock and did what he could to prevent mercury and mine drainage from washing into Marsh Creek and the Delta.

“It’s hard to require someone who never did any mining to clean up the whole area,” said Mitch Avalon, deputy public works director for Contra Costa County.

Wessman may now be getting some help. Under the federal Superfund Law, the Environmental Protection Agency is tracing the history of the mine to identify who is responsible for cleaning up the mess.

There’s a long way to go, but one oil company has come forward and fixed a dam that was in imminent danger of failing. Had the dam collapsed, mercury-laden water would have spilled into Marsh Creek, which drains into the Delta.

One of Contra Costa County’s claim to fame is it has the first female deputy sheriff in California. The deputy was Leila Veale. After the election in which women in California won the right to vote, Sheriff Richard Veale, who was sheriff for 40 years, asked Governor Hiram Johnson for permission to appoint his daughter as a deputy sheriff.

Among her duties, the new deputy sheriff was charged with cooking meals for the jailers and the prisoners. Deputy Leila received no pay.

Contra Costa was one of the original 27 counties in California, created in 1850 at the time of statehood. The county was originally called Mt. Diablo County. Contra Costa, in Spanish, means opposite coast.

Del Norte County

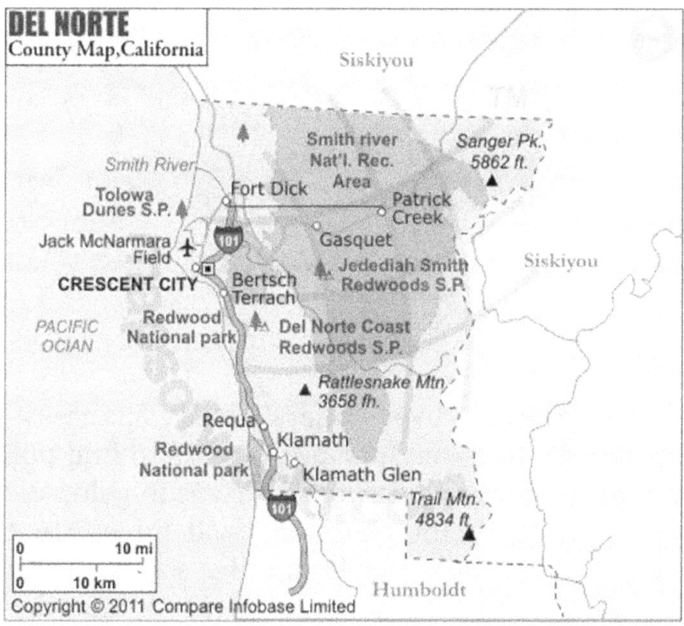

Map of Del Norte County

Jedediah Smith was the first European American to explore this land and the first to reach the area overland on foot in a time before the Europeans even knew about the distant territory.

Between 1880 and 1990, Del Norte County produced approximately 50,000 ounces of placer gold and 1,000 ounces of lode gold.

Diamond Creek had several lode mines. The Keystone mine was a lode mine in the Rockland district.

The Smith River Forks

Monkey Creek is said to contain placer gold as is Shelly Creek.

The Smith River offers good chances for recreational and amateur prospectors to find placer gold. Most of its tributaries also contain gold.

Del Norte County had 431 gold mines. In Del Norte County, granite forms the nucleus of the mountain ranges and over it is a mantle of metamorphic rocks.

Fine particle gold can be found on the Del Norte County beaches. The Smith River also has placer gold deposits.

On the south fork of the Smith River, which had large scale dredging operations, is Coon Creek. Gold may found in the cemented gravels of the creek and on gravel bars.

El Dorado County

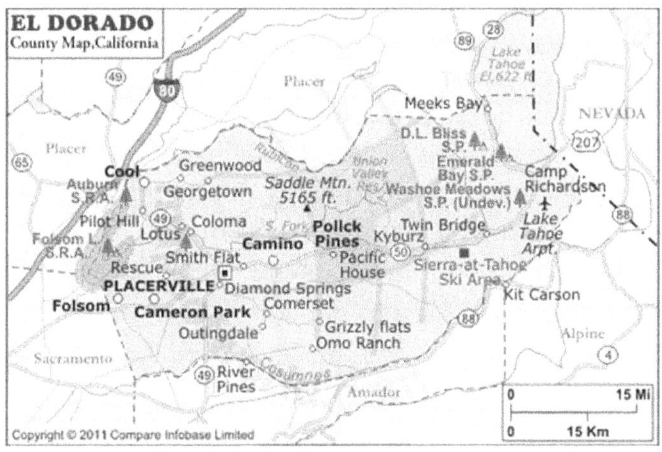

Map of El Dorado County

El Dorado means "Gilded One" in Spanish. The town of El Dorado was originally called Mud Springs. It was the site of rich placer diggings.

It is in this county that James Marshall discovered gold at Coloma in1848 on the South Fork of the American River.

Despite notices from the state and at least $100,000 in fines, a small team of outlaw miners is continuing to illegally excavate an abandoned gold mine near Placerville in El Dorado County.

The team returne certified letters and notices of violation unopened and ignores fines levied by the State Mining and Geology Board. The mining at Big Cut Mine continues.

The miners in violation bought the property in 2006. But they have been in violation of state and local laws for years by not getting proper permits or permission to mine.

Big Cut Mine was historically mined for gold but was abandoned during World War II when the federal government ordered its closure.

Many placer operations were conducted along the American River and its tributaries.

Near the town of Placerville there are many old placer mines that exist near all local streams.

Coloma

Recreational gold seekers should try Coloma where gold panning demonstrations and lessons are given at the Marshal Gold Discovery Park.

Pilot Hill

At Pilot Hill, A.J. Bayley built the Bayley House in anticipation of serving passengers from the Central Pacific Railroad. It sits near Highway 49 in the tiny Pilot Hill community.

It has become known as “Bayley’s Folly”. It was used as the first Grange Hall in California.

Georgetown

Georgetown was started by George Phipps and some sailors who discovered gold there. It was originally called Growlersburg because gold pans were said to "growl" with nuggets.

Diamond Springs

Diamond Springs was one of the richest spots in the area. It is located on the Carson Emigrant Trail. To the east of Diamond Springs is Shingle Springs, named for its cool spring that flowed near a shingle mill.

Fresno County

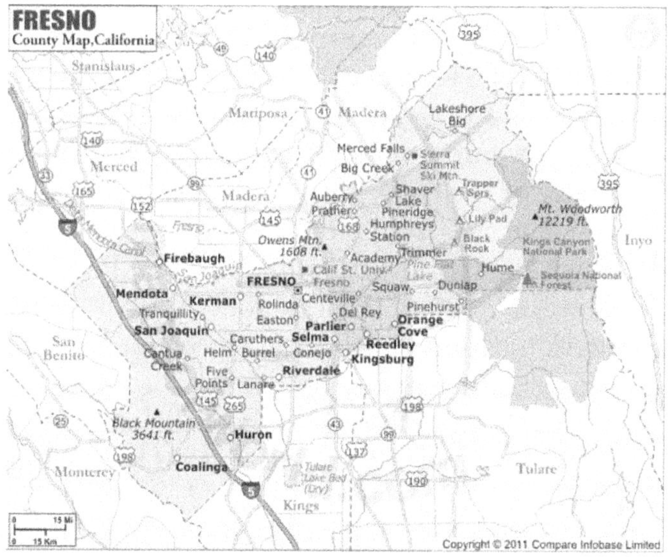

Fresno County Map

Fresno County was once a dry desert. It came into being during a search for a suitable mission site. The county was created in 1856. The first county seat was located at the foothill community of Millerton.

When a railroad line was developed through the valley, the town of Fresno was created. The town took its name from the ash trees native to the valley. (Fresno is the Spanish word for "ash tree").

A good place for gold seekers to start is at the Coarsegold Historic Village. Here, Rattlesnake

Rick, a local gold panning expert, helps people get their hands wet in a special area set up for panning. Panners get to keep the gold they find.

Coarsegold

The town of Coarsegold got its name from the coarse chunks of gold in the area's streams and rivers in the mid-1800s. The town once reached a population of 10,000, but when the gold petered out, the town was relegated to becoming a stop for travelers heading for Yosemite National Park.

Coarsegold Gold Prospectors is a nonprofit organization that offers monthly events for gold-prospecting enthusiasts.

After gold was discovered in California, miners flocked to the foothill areas of the San Joaquin River.

Placer gravels along the San Joaquin River produced 121,000 ounces of gold between 1880 and 1959. At the Friant Dam, the gravel excavated to use in building the dam produced $196,977 in placer gold between the years 1940-42.

Glenn County

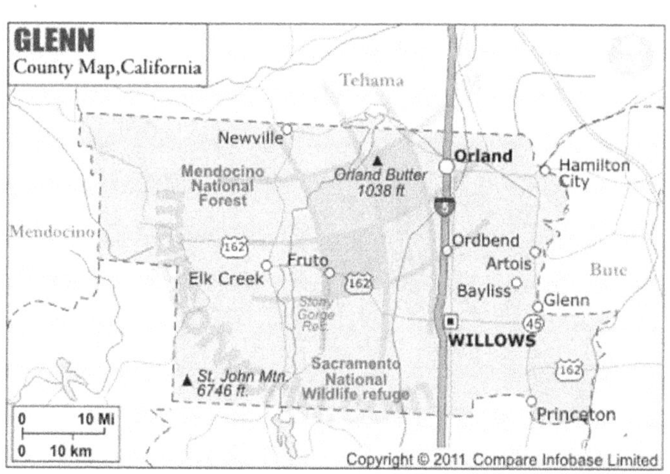

Map of Glenn County

Glenn County was formed in 1891 from parts of Colusa County. It was named for Hugh J. Glenn, the largest wheat farmer in the state.

The county has a total area of 1,327 square miles, of which 1314 square miles is land and 13 square miles is water.

This county was formed after the initial Gold Rush. No literature on gold panning in Glenn County was available.

Humboldt County

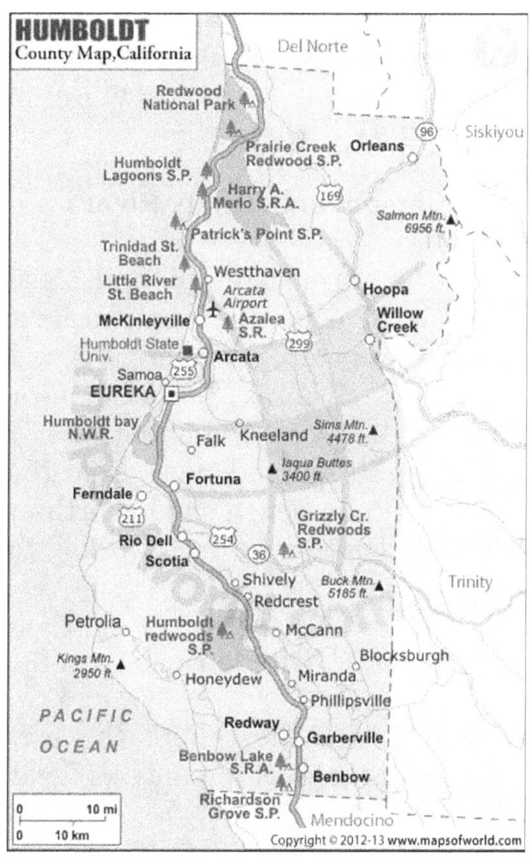

Humboldt County Map

The first recorded exploration of California's northern coast was at Trinidad by the Spanish in 1775. The first to enter Humboldt Bay occurred in 1806, when Aleut hunters in the employ of the

Russian-American Company in Sitka entered the bay.

In 1850, ships brought their passengers to Humboldt and Trinidad bays, where men believed to be from the United States disembarked and headed to the mining districts on the Klamath, Salmon and Trinity Rivers.

Klamath and Trinity Rivers

Gold is the principal mineral resource of Humboldt County, primarily from placers along the Klamath and Trinity Rivers. There are six lode gold mines shown on U.S. Forest Service quadrangles.

It's known that the Klamath River contains placer gold along its entire length. Near the town of Orick, the area ocean beach sands north and south of the Klamath River was once worked for placer gold and platinum.

Trinidad

There are stories that claim the ocean itself washed up thousands of pounds of gold on the beach of Trinidad.

In those years, it was generally said that almost any man of good enterprise and muscle could take his hat and a wheelbarrow and gather up enough gold to last him a year or two.

It was this excitement that led to the settlement of the county. It wasn't all good. It made people dissatisfied with everyday affairs and created a gambling craze.

Some reports indicate that Humboldt County may have a new era of placer mining if modern methods of looking for the black sand containing platinum are put to use.

Gold Bluffs beach which was one of the richest of the placers in Humboldt County.

Gold has been found in every part of the county extending from Dobyn's Creek to the Trinity section and Scott's Bar.

There are raging stories about miners who flocked into the area in 1850. Many expected to find all the supplies they needed on the river. Very few small trains arrived with supplies and the provisions were soon eaten up and there was a crowd of several thousand men without anything to eat.

One story is told about a man who was able to kill two grouse. He was offered $8 each for them. He declined to sell them as he needed them for himself.

At last a supply train got through to Salmon Creek and found a hearty welcome among the half-starved miners.

Hundreds of men who had been snowed in made their way over the mountains to Orleans Bar. They suffered great hardships along the way and reached those places almost famished.

Gold Bluffs

In the days of the early gold excitement, Gold Bluffs was one of the most notoriously rich of all the placers. It is located on the beach, twenty-five miles north of Trinidad and nine miles south of the mouth of the Klamath River.

Imperial County

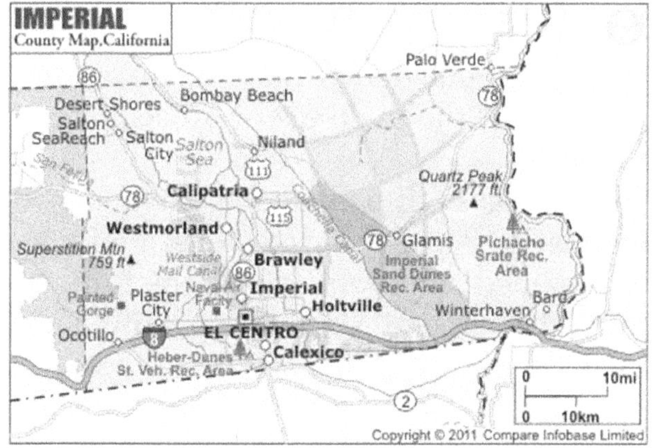

Map of Imperial County

Tumco is an abandoned gold mining town and is also one of the earliest gold mining areas in California. It is located 25 miles from Yuma, Arizona north of Highway 80.

This is all that left of Tumco

A railroad track walker named Hedges made a gold find there in the early 1880s. The excitement lured 3,000 persons to the site, which was then called Hedges.

Water was piped in from the Colorado River. Hedges had all the makings of a boomtown except for a hotel.

When Hedges felt he had enough money, he sold his holdings to Borden, the condensed milk baron.

He renamed the town, taking the initials of the company (The United Mining Company) and called the town Tumco.

Gold occurs in Imperial County in its arid mountain ranges. Here is where the classic image of the pick, pan, shovel and burro prospector of the nineteenth century originated.

Ogilby

Northwest of Yuma, Arizona, in the southwest part of Imperial County, the Ogilby site of the Cargo Muchacho district is located. Gold can be found in all regional arroyo bottoms, benches and terraces.

This is dry-wash placers with abundant gold. Abandoned lode gold mines dot the area. The Chocolate Mountains area has placer and lode claims that produce considerable gold.

Inyo County

Inyo County Map

Inyo is the second largest county in California, comprising 10,135 square miles. The highest point in the County is Mt. Whitney and the lowest point is Badwater, Death Valley.

Inyo County owes much of its development to an incident that occurred in the winter of 1849-1850.

In 1849, a group of California-bound emigrants headed out from Utah 107 wagons led by Captain Jefferson Hunt. The group disagreed on the most direct route to the gold fields.

Some believed there was a much shorter route across the desert rather than taking the Old Spanish Trail. Wagon Master Hunt warned that crossing the desert was “walking into the jaws of hell”.

Several members parted near Enterprise, Utah, believing the shortcut would save them 20 days of travel. This group became known as the “Lost 49’ers”.

Before reaching White Sage Flat, the party split again. One group hiked over the Panamint Mountains and the other took the floor of the desert.

The two parties met up again at White Sage Flat. Jim Martin, one of the travelers, showed a piece of silver ore he found while crossing the mountains.

The Panamint Mountains

Exhausted, starving and some near death, the travelers were little interested in Martin’s bit of mineral ore.

The pioneers had killed six oxen for meat, burned their wagons, and were forced to walk most of the way on what was supposed to be a shortcut.

After four months, the travelers stumbled into Mariposa, glad to say goodbye to Death Valley.

After getting settled, Jim Martin, who had lost the sight off his rifle during the trip, took his piece of silver ore to a gunsmith who made it into a new rifle sight.

The gunsmith could keep the story quiet. He quickly spread the story about the legend of the Lost Gunsight Mine.

Ballarat

In the Ballarat area, many old mine dumps show gold traces. The Ratcliff Mine was a chief producer of lode gold.

Seventeen miles west of Bishop is the Willshire-Bishop Creek district. The Bishop Creek Mine and the Willshire Mine were large lode gold producers.

At Death Valley National Monument, on a slope of the Funeral Range, is the Chloride Cliff district. It had a production of 60,000 ounces of gold.

East of Lone Pine the Reward and Brown Monster mines were major lode gold producers.

The Wild Rose gold district lies in the Panamint Mountains. It produced 73,000 ounces of gold from the Skidoo Mine.

Kern County

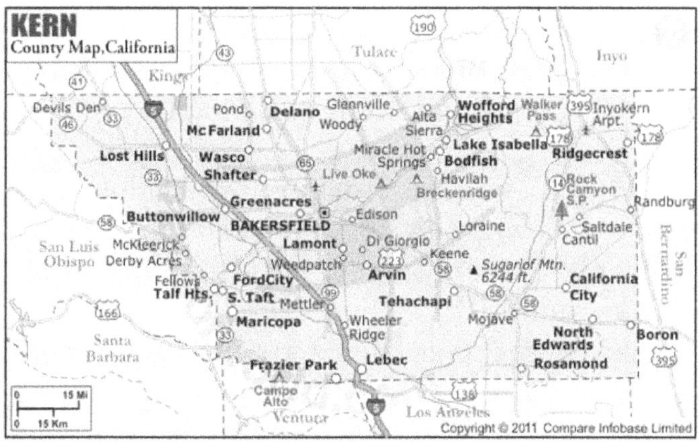

Kern County Map

Kern County is Southern California's "Golden County". If a gold rush in the California desert is eminent, it will manifest itself in Kern County first.

The area was first claimed by the Spanish in 1769. In 1772, Commander Don Pedro Fages became the first European to enter it.

Kern County was the site of the Battle of San Emigdio in March 1824. The battle was between the Chumash Indians of the Santa Barbara Mission and the Mexican government.

It was a low casualty encounter with four Indians killed and no Mexicans. The surviving Indians were brought back to Santa Barbara.

What is now Kern County was dominated by mining in the mountains and in the desert. A county government was established in 1866. The

County Seat was in the mining town of Havilah, in the mountains between Bakersfield and Tehachapi.

The flatlands were considered inhospitable and impassable due to swaps, lakes and tule reeds. Diseases, such as malaria were also a problem.

Randsburg and Mojave

Gold mines in Randsburg and Mojave were considered low-grade 40 years ago when gold was worth only $35 an ounce and silver less than one dollar an ounce.

These desert gold mines are not considered low-grade anymore. Kern County gold mining is expected to pick up its pace in the future, depending on economic conditions.

While placer gold is abundant in Kern County, there is a lack of water to assist in recovery of the gold. It's predicted that a few lucky individuals could make fortunes in Kern County during the next gold rush.

Kings County

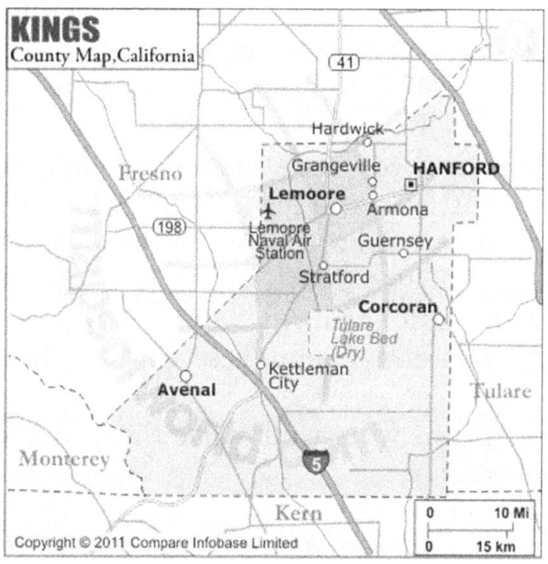

Map of Kings County

An 1805 expedition led by Spanish Army Lieutenant Gabriel Moraga discovered the River and named it *El Rio de Los Santos Reyes* (River of the Holy Kings). The name refers to the Three Wise Men of the Bible.

After the United States' conquest over Mexico, the River name was changed to Kings River, which later became the name of the county as well.

In 1880, there was a dispute over land tiles between the settlers and the Southern Pacific Railroads. The event was the Mussel Slough Tragedy.

This incident occurred seven miles northwest of Hanford. Seven men died.

The fight was spawned when Congress voted to give the Southern Pacific Company a huge land grant to help subsidize a rail line. If the company met the terms of the grant, it could then sell the "odd-numbered" sections to cover its costs.

The land prices were low enough to encourage people to settle in the arid Mussel Slough district. The settled area grew to four thousand people.

In the 1870s, Southern Pacific stunned the settlers by announcing it would charge a market value of $20 to $25 an acre for the homestead lands.

These prices were well above those stated in the pamphlets.

When settlement attempts failed, six hundred Mussel Slough residents formed the Settlers' League. While initially nonviolent, the League's approach shifted after Southern Pacific brought suit.

Masked vigilantes rode through the district at night, intimidating residents who sided with the railroad. The situation became even tenser when Southern Pacific brought suits of ejectment against twenty three members of the Settlers' League.

During a picnic sponsored by the Settlers' League, Southern Pacific sent U.S. Marshal Alonzo Poole, land appraiser Walter Clark, and residents Walter Crow and Mills Hartt to dispossess several settlers.

The railroad men were outnumbered. Within minutes an argument ensued, followed by a burst of gunfire. Hartt and five settlers were killed. Crow initially escaped but was killed by an unknown gunman.

Tensions did ease some. Some settlers purchased the lands they occupied but many did not.

Mussel Slough was renamed Lucerne Valley.

Lake County

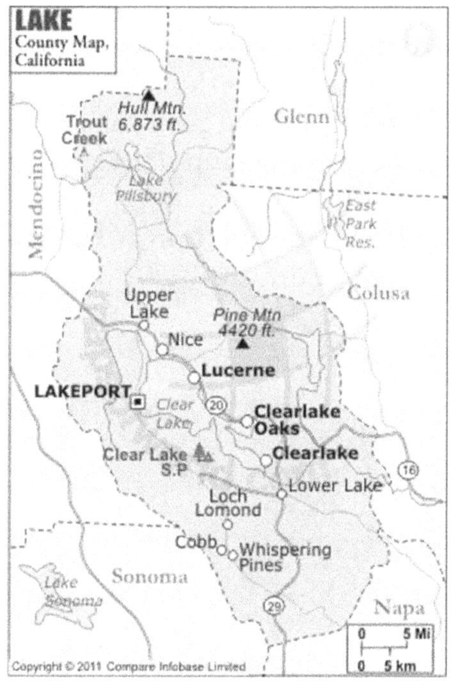

Lake County Map

Lake County is walled in with Mount St. Helena on one side, Mayacamas on the west and Hull Mountain and San Hedron Mountain on the north.

The county was formed from land taken from Napa County and from Mendocino County.

Pioneers began arriving in the valley in 1845. They were mostly cowboys herding cattle for General Mariano Vallejo.

The county is named for Clear Lake, said to be the oldest lake in North America due to a geological fluke. The lake sits on a huge block of stone which slowly tilts in the northern direction at the same rate as the lake fills in with sediment, thus keep the water at the same depth.

Mount Konocti, the largest volcano in the Clear Lake volcanic field, rises up 4,299 feet above Clear Lake.

Little if any information exists about gold panning in Lake County.

Lassen County

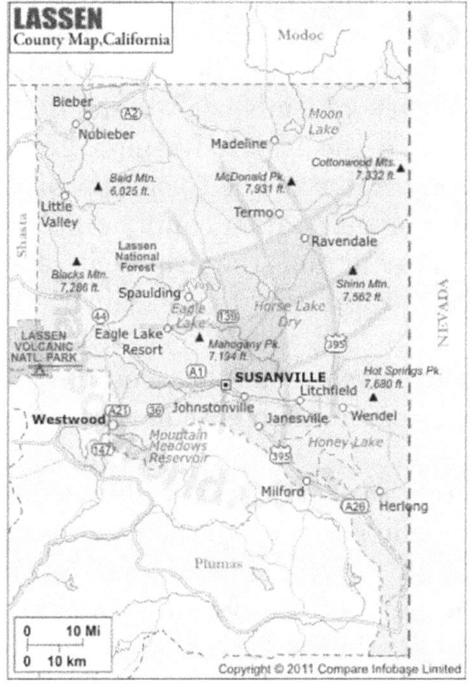

Lassen County Map

Peter Lassen was one of Honey Lake Valley's first residents. He was born in Denmark. It was Danish custom to have a last name based on his father's first name. Peter was born to Lars Nielson and Johanne Sophie.

Another resident of Honey Valley was Isaac Roop. Isaac established a trading post where travelers along the Nobles Emigrant Trail could stock up on provisions before crossing the Sierra Nevada.

It was first known as *Rooptown*, It later became Susanville, named for Roop's daughter.

Residents of Susanville were unhappy with Plumas County officials who wanted to levy and collect taxes in the isolated region. In 1856, Isaac Roop and Peter Lassen led a group of disgruntled citizens in a revolt against county officials.

Roop, Lassen and the irate citizens opted to form a separate territory, which they called *Nataqua*.

The short-lived republic was largely ignored because the region affected had only a few hundred settlers.

When the Territory of Nevada was established, Roop was made governor of the new territory. A few years later, a survey showed that Susanville was actually a part of California. Thus, the County Lassen was established.

In 1863, the quiet little town of Susanville was disturbed by the sound of gunfire. Forces from Roop County Nevada and Plumas California battled for control of the Honey Lake Region.

Finally, a new survey was ordered. It was determined that the town of Aurora was in Nevada and that Susanville and Honey Lake were in California.

Unable to accept this situation, Honey Lake residents gained independence from Plumas County and formed Lassen County. The County Seat was in Susanville.

Gold production from Lassen County has come primarily from the Diamond Mountain and Hayden Hill districts.

Diamond Mountain is located six miles south of Susanville.

In the early days, most of the gold production came from placer deposits. Later, production came most from lode deposits.

The Hayden Hill district is in the north-central portion of Lassen County. Most of the gold all came from lode mines.

Gold seekers can pan for gold at the Rich Bar Mining Co., which will even supply the hand tools in covered panning booths. Rich Bar Mining Co. is located 24 miles west of Quincy off Highway 70.

At the Golden Caribou Mining Club, free gold panning lessons are offered to first time visitors. The club has 2,000 acres of gold mining claims and offers lifetime memberships.

Gold panning is also available on public national forest lands that have not been staked. Popular spots are the Middle Fork of the Feather River, Wapunsie Creek off of the Snake Lake Road, Spanish Creek, and the Lakes Basin Recreational Area.

Los Angeles County

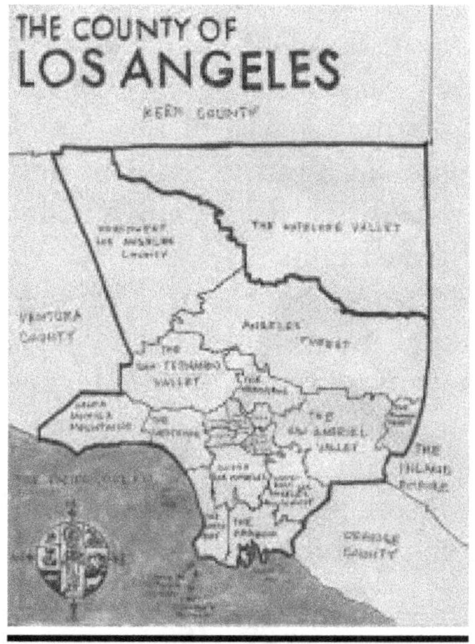

The *Los Angeles Pobladores* (townspeople) is the name given the 44 original settlers in Los Angeles. There were 22 adults and 22 children.

In May 1846, the Mexican-American War began. Because Mexico was unable to defend its northern territories, California was exposed to invasion.

Commodore Robert F. Stockton and John C. Fremont seized the town. Governor Pico fled to Mexico.

After three weeks of occupation, Stockton left, leaving Lieutenant Archibald H. Gillespie in charge. Gillespie and his troops treated the Mexican residents harshly.

Finally, a local force of 300 forced the Americans to leave, ending the first phase of the Battle of Los Angeles.

San Gabriel River

A short distance north of Los Angeles is a very productive gold area in the San Gabriel Range.

The San Gabriel River has yielded promising amounts of placer gold.

Prospectors in Southern California say the severe drought has exposed gold that has never been touched by man. As water levels drop, more nooks and crannies are easier to access.

Where once only the husband or head of the family was seen prospecting, now entire families are joining the search.

Lytle Creek

Prospectors at Lytle Creek use sluice boxes and metal detectors. Armed with simple equipment, amateur as well as seasoned prospectors can find it worth their while to hunt the elusive metal.

One gold seeker is not so enchanted. He said, "I've been three times up and down the river and never found anything but rusty nails and bottle caps."

Another prospector said, "Droughts don't cause gold rushes. Bad economies do."

Some of the prospectors focus on more of the remote streams which have not been worked as thoroughly as those near a paved road.

Madera County

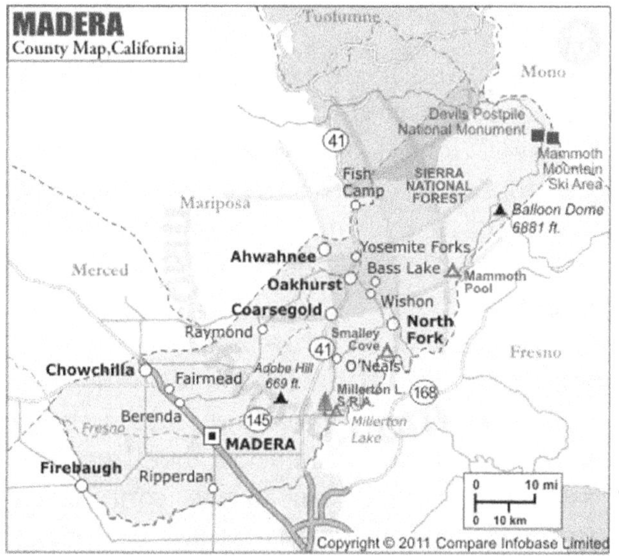

Madera County Map

"Madera" is the Spanish word for "lumber", the first industry for the county. A huge flume once ran from the high Sierra down to Madera. It was considered an engineering marvel of early California.

The discovery of gold brought the first big wave of immigrants. Most of them were placer miners working the streams that were rich in precious metal.

Records indicate that county resident Jim Savage hired Chinese laborers to work the San Joaquin River. Savage was previously known for "fighting the Indians" but as the population grew, he made friends with them, even to the extent of marrying at least five Indian girls, one from each tribe.

The oldest and most extensively worked was an area called Coarsegold.

Charles Michael is believed to be the first resident to arrive in the area. He began raising cattle and sheep to feed the gold miners. In 1878, the first post office was established called "Coarse Gold Gulch".

In 1889, the community of Coarsegold Gulch boasted of the St. Charles Hotel (20 rooms), a general merchandise store, a blacksmith shop, a saloon and dance hall, and a few dwellings.

Coarsegold is still an active community and treasure hunters still find gold dust and nuggets in nearby streams.

Marin County

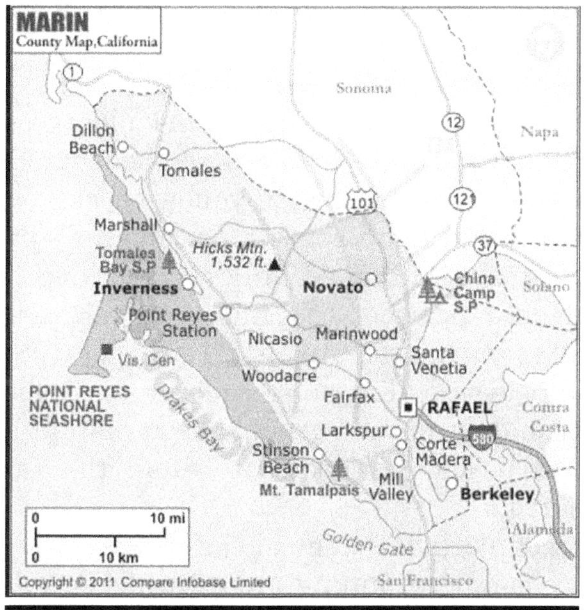

Marin County Map

Marin was the name of a famous Indian Chief of the Lacatuit Indian tribe. After vanquishing the Spaniards in several skirmishes, Marin was captured.

In making his escape, he took shelter on a small island in the bay of San Francisco. The chief was captured a second time. He barely escaped being put to death through the interference of the priests at the mission in San Rafael.

Marin died at the mission in 1834.

In 1896, the *San Francisco Call* reported gold was found in Sausalito Creek. According to the article, John Hayes, a police sergeant for the Board of Harbor Commissioners, had a creek in the back of his residence.

Hayes and some friends did some casual panning in the creek. They found plenty of black sand and when the dirt was washed out of their pans, there were four bright yellow specks.

They found more gold on an adjoining property owned by a man named Miller. The group decided that before news of the find was released, they needed to buy up the property.

Miller was willing to sell his property for $250. Unfortunately for the group, the news did get out and Miller learned about it before the sale was completed.

Sergeant Hayes went ahead in his effort to set up a cooperative mining group, which would have included Miller. No further news reports were forthcoming on his efforts.

Sir Francis Drake explored the area around 1775. The chronicler for Drake's voyage wrote: "The earth of the country seemed to promise rich veins of gold and silver, some of the ore being constantly found on digging."

Mariposa County

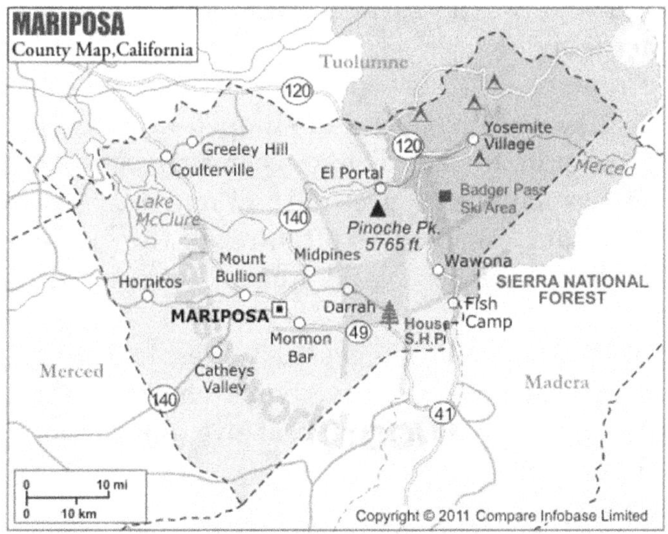

Mariposa County Map

While the legislature was awaiting statehood in 1850, it created the structure of the new state. It made Mariposa the largest county covering one-fifth of the state.

The legislature's intent is not clear, but it is assumed that because the area south of Mariposa was largely waste land. At that time there were only 11 counties.

John C. Fremont and his wife Jessie bought a 44,000-acre land grant, *Las Mariposa*, from Juan Bautista Alvarado, the last Mexican governor of California.

It was thought by the local people that Fremont's purchase only included the grazing and agricultural rights. Fremont knew that under American law, the surface owner also controlled the mineral rights.

Fremont and his wife Jessie began operating a gold mine at Mariposa and shipped hundred pound bags of gold to San Francisco for processing. The mine provided the source of the Fremont's fortune.

Amateur prospectors often recall the excitement of finding that first gold nugget or even fleck of gold.

Here are some suggested places to try to find gold in Mariposa County. Some charge a fee and others are free. Some places give instructions on gold panning.

Briceburg Recreation Area

Briceburg Recreation Area is located about 15 miles east of Mariposa on Highway 140. Some gold panning places may not have all the equipment you need, so you might want to bring your own gold panning equipment. Don't forget the water and something to eat as some places are remote.

Bagby Recreation Area

In the Bagby Recreational Area, located 15 miles north of Mariposa on Highway 49, you can pan for gold for a nominal fee.

Coulterville and Greeley Hill also have several likely spots to pan for gold. One suggestion is to drop into the Magnolia Bar of the Jeffery Hotel and have a beer and chat with the locals.

Mendocino County

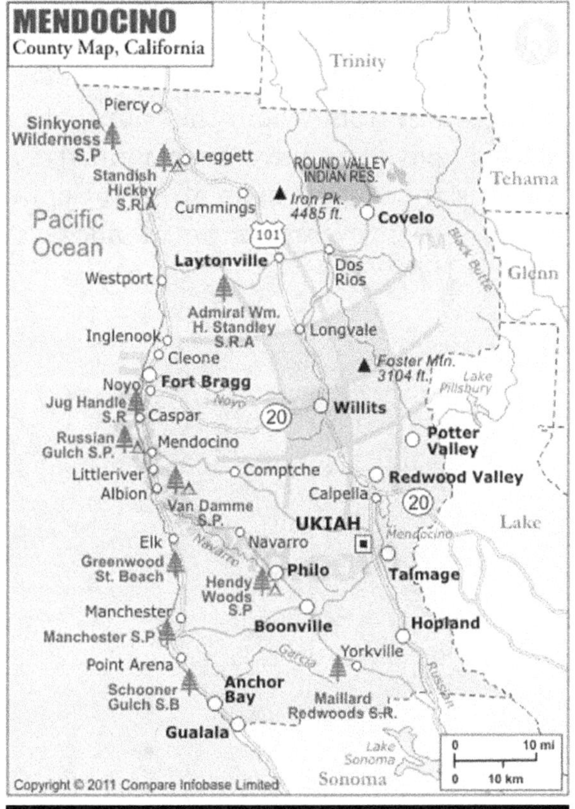

Mendocino County Map

Mineral production in Mendocino County has been small. In 1919, some $14,214 worth of gold was harvested, ranking fifty-first among the counties.

Mendocino County was one of the original counties of California created in 1850 at the time of Statehood. It had few people populating the county and didn't have a separate government until 1859. Until then, it was under the administration of Sonoma County.

It is uncertain from whom the county derived its name. It is believed to have been named for either Antonio de Mendoza, Viceroy of New Spain, 1535-1542 or for Lorenzo Suarez de Mendoza, Viceroy from 1580 to 1583.

Merced County

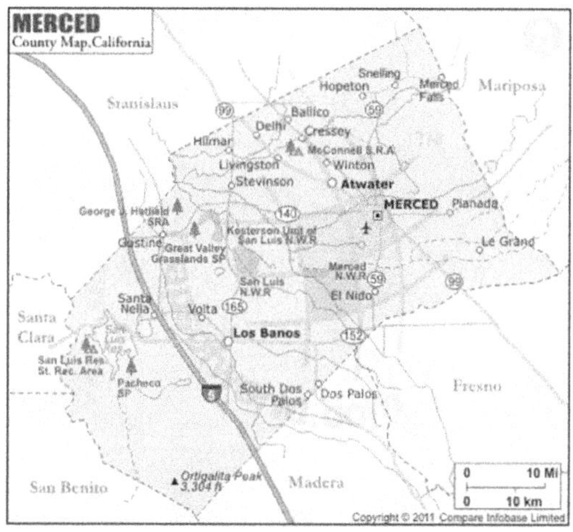

Merced County Map

The foothills between Merced County and Yosemite were a part of the Mother Lode known as the "Southern Mines". The line separating them from the Northern Mines was drawn along the Mokelumne River, a few miles south of Jackson.

Merced Falls and Snelling

Merced County has produced considerable gold from one general locality, the alluvial plain between Merced Falls and Snelling. In 1907, the Yosemite Mining and Dredging Company operated the first connected bucket dredges in the Snelling area.

The War Production Board Order L-208 of 1942, along with rising costs and resoiling ordinances, all contributed to a decline in large scale dredging and gold mining in Merced County.

Modoc County

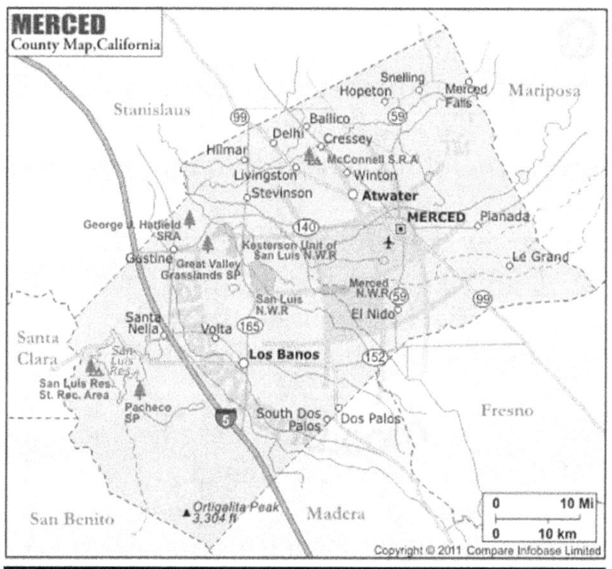

Modoc County Map

Located in the far northeast corner of California, Modoc County is the third-least populous county in California.

The Modoc Indian War was one of the costliest of the nineteenth century. It developed from a misunderstanding between the Modoc Indians and the United States Army.

In 1864, the Modocs signed a treaty with the United States where they would receive goods and protection if they moved to the Klamath Indian Reservation in Oregon.

U.S. Indian agency officials ignored Modoc grievances. This sent two hundred Modocs into an uprising. Under the leadership of Kintpuash (Captain Jack), they fled the Klamath reservation, resettling along Lost River, their ancestral home.

There were a number of events leading up to the Modoc War. The first known explorers in Modoc country were John Charles Fremont and his scout, Kit Carson.

Carson awakened in the night to the sound of a thump. Leaping up, he saw his friend and fellow trapper, Basil Lajeunesse sprawled in blood. Carson alerted the camp that they were under attack by Indians.

By the time the attackers were beaten back, two more of Fremont's group fell dead.

In an effort to avenge the deaths, the rash Fremont attacked a Klamath tribe fishing village. The attack destroyed the village and women and children, as well as warriors, were killed.

Historians believe Fremont and Carson chose the wrong tribe in their vengeful attack. The attack on the explorers probably came from the Modoc tribe. The Klamath tribe and the Modoc tribe were bitter enemies.

Captain Jack and his Modoc followers moved back to the Klamath reservation three times between 1865 and 1869. Each time, they were treated poorly by Indian agents. They fled again, settling along Lost River, their ancestral home.

President Ulysses Grant gave orders to force the Modocs back to the Klamath reservation. Under a cavalry commanded by Captain James Jackson, the army opened fire on Kintpuash's camp. The Modocs were forced to flee to the Lava Beds in northern California.

Captain Jack, leader of the Modocs

Over the next two months, three major battles occurred as U.S. troops attempted to get inside the Lava Beds and attack the Modocs.

President Grant then appointed a peace commission, led by General Edward R.S. Canby. Canby was to meet with the Modocs and persuade them to return to the Klamath reservation.

Canby sent two primary interpreters, Winema "Toby" Riddle and her husband Frank Riddle to visit the Lava Beds. Winema returned with the warning that the Modocs intended to kill the peace commissioners if they did not comply with Modoc demands.

Among their demands was a reservation along Lost River and exoneration for the previous murders of settlers.

Canby ignored Winema's warnings and proceeded with a meeting with Captain Jack. Captain Jack and his advisors tried to negotiate, but Canby refused to listen. Captain Canby demanded their unconditional surrender.

The Modocs carried out their warnings, killing Canby, Reverend Eleasar Thomas and L.S. Dyar. Alfred Meacham was wounded.

Four battles followed, bringing the army closer to the Modocs' stronghold, forcing them to disperse. Captain Jack surrendered. He and five other Modocs stood trial and were sentenced to hang.

The government exiled the remaining 153 Modocs to Indian Territory.

Though Modoc County was never known as prime mining country, a few treasure tales are told. A sheepherder is said to have picked up a heavy rock on the west slope of the South Warner Mountains. He forgot about the stone for several months.

He finally took it to an assayer. He was appropriately shocked when told that the rock was almost pure gold. An Alturas banker grubstaked the sheepherder, who returned to the area, but was never able to find the rock source again.

Mono County

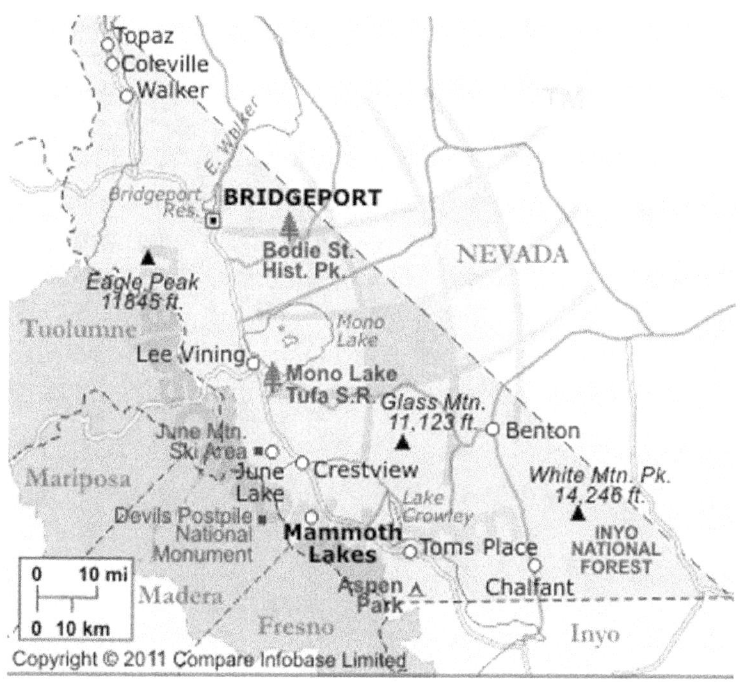

Mono County Map

Archeologists know little about the first inhabitants of Mono County. The Kuzedika, a band of the Paiute, has been there for many generations.

Mining began in Mono County 1862 when silver was discovered at Blind Springs Hill. Gold mining came later. The most important lode districts were Bodie and Masonic.

Bodie State Historic Park is a genuine California gold-mining ghost town. In 1875, a mine caved in and revealed rich pay dirt. People flocked to Bodie, creating a boomtown.

Small amounts of placer gold were found near the headwaters of Walker River, along Virginia Creek, and Dog Creek.

Dog Town was the site of the first major gold rush to the eastern slope of the Sierra Nevada. Dog Town got its name from a popular miner's term for camps with huts or hovels. Dog Town's remains are located on Highway 395, seven miles south of Bridgeport.

Scattered mines in the Casa Diablo Mountains have produced less than $1 million in gold and silver.

Monterey County

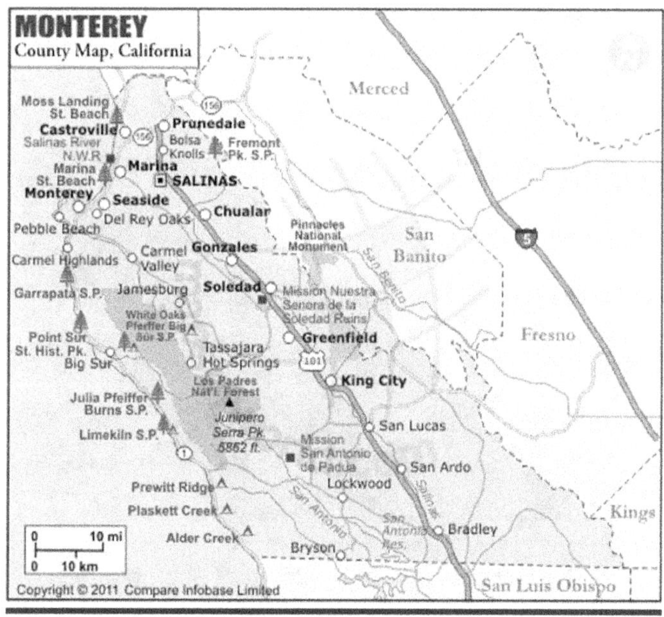

Monterey County Map

David Jack arrived in Monterey in 1850. He involved himself in the settlement of Mexican Land claims. When the city of Monterey could not pay a one thousand dollar legal bill, its lands were auctioned.

Jack and Delos Rodeyn Ashley, the attorney representing Monterey in its legal problems, bought the entire tract for $2002.50. In 1869, Ashley turned his interest in the land over to Jack.

This meant that Jack now owned the cities of Monterey, Pacific Grove, Seaside, and Del Rey Oaks, along with Del Monte Forest (Now known as Pebble Beach). He also owned Fort Ord.

The Gem Saloon in the town of Manchester

Not long after the Cruikshank gold discovery near Alder Creek, several hundred miners staked claims. The town of Manchester, sometimes called Mansfield, was born.

The south Monterey County town acquired a post office in 1889 under the name of Manchester. The town had a hotel, two general stores, a barber shop, a restaurant and the post office. In addition there was a one-room school, a blacksmith shop, mess halls and bunkhouses, and a small cemetery.

While the town had all of these amenities, there was no road to the town. The town burned to the ground in the 1890s.

To get to the former site of Manchester requires traveling eight miles on a steep, gnarly uphill dirt road to the Coast Ridge summit. Then it requires going another couple of miles on even steeper, rockier and much less traveled road down the far side of ridge to Alder Creek. Don't even think of going there in wet weather.

Some small area mines in the Los Burros district have contained quartz veins and lode gold.

Most of the properties are near the government mail trail between Jolon, east of San Antonio River, and Gorda, a small ranching development midway between Monterey and San Luis Obispo.

Napa County

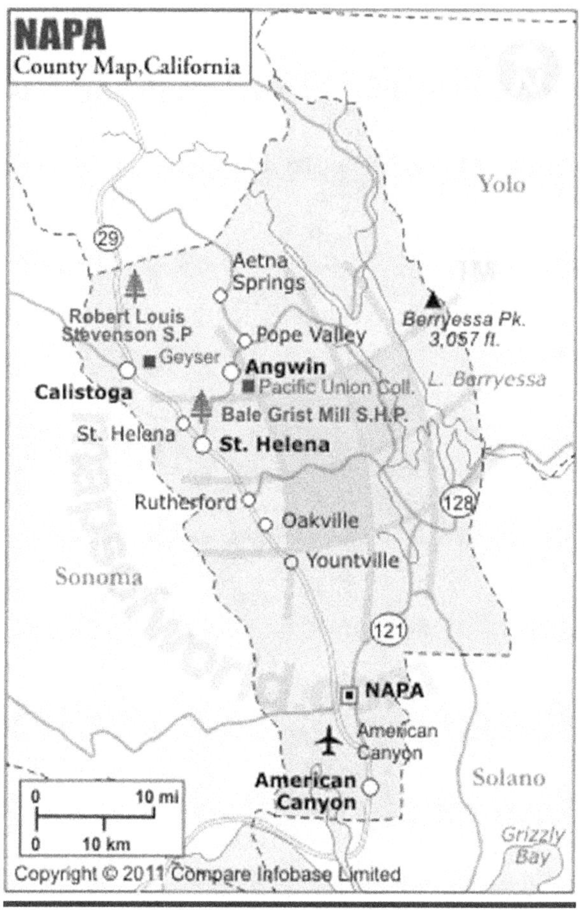

Napa County came late to the Gold Rush. From 1985 to 2002, Homestake Mining Company extracted $1 billion worth of gold from the desolate landscape above Lake Berryessa.

Prospectors have roamed the area. Generally, they've some silver, but all the gold was hidden from view. There were no nuggets are glittery gold veins.

Homestake Mining Co. blasted to 900 feet below the surface in search of gold. One hundred and fifty tons of rocks, of which 38 million tons are said to have contained gold, were crushed.

Nevada County

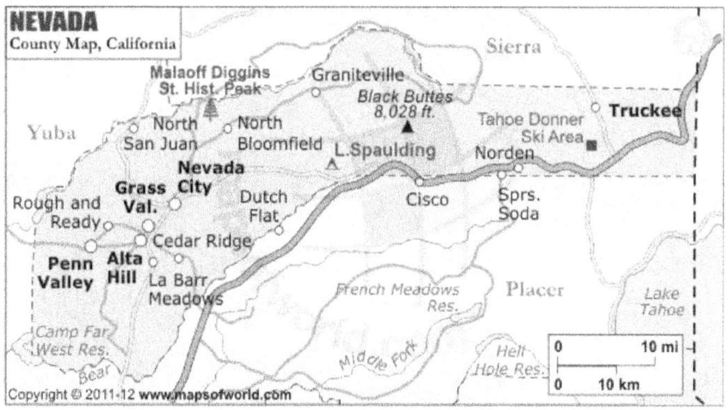

Nevada County Map

Pioneers who crossed the Sierra Nevada before the snows fell often rested at Greenhorn Creek near present-day Nevada City.

One of Grass Valley's most famous residents was Lola Montez, who performed her famous "spider dance" to audiences around the world. Her dance imitated a woman who had spiders climbing within her petticoats.

Montez married three times, once to Ludwig 1, the King of Bavaria.

After marrying her third husband, Patrick Hull, they bought a house in "Grass Valley". It was the only home she ever owned. She lived there from 1853 until 1855.

When the pioneers first arrived in what is now Grass Valley, their cattle wandered, seeking out the lush grasses in the meadows. The miner's dubbed the area "the grassy valley".

There are 16 major gold mines in the Nevada City area. When gold was found in Deer Creek, Nevada City became the largest and wealthiest mining town in California.

Nevada City was originally a mining camp founded along Deer Creek. It became the largest and wealthiest mining town in California. At one time, Nevada City was the third largest city in California with a population of 10,000 people.

In the neighboring town of Grass Valley, it is believed that millions of dollars in gold still likes buried deep in the earth.

By 1855, Grass Valley was still growing when fire swept through the city destroying 300 buildings.

After rebuilding, the town faced a worse disaster. Finding gold was getting more and more difficult. Hard rock mining allowed Grass Valley to bounce back and once again prosper from gold mining by the 1860s.

Unfortunately, miners used hydraulic mining techniques, washing away the hillsides. Miners also introduced tons of mercury into the environment to extract the gold.

Nevada City, working with both federal and local partners, are assessing five major mine tailings areas in the heart of the city for cleanup.

Both placer and lode gold mines operated in Nevada County beginning in 1850.

While many placer deposits are known to be rich today, they have not been touched today because of state laws ending hydraulic mining.

Both Nevada City and Grass Valley have historic mining architecture and provide wonderful places for tourists.

Some of the most accessible gold panning locations are on the South Yuba River at Bridgeport, Edwards Crossing and Washington. On the Middle Yuba River gold may be found at Oregon Creek.

There are public sections of the river open and claim jumping isn't a problem.

Orange County

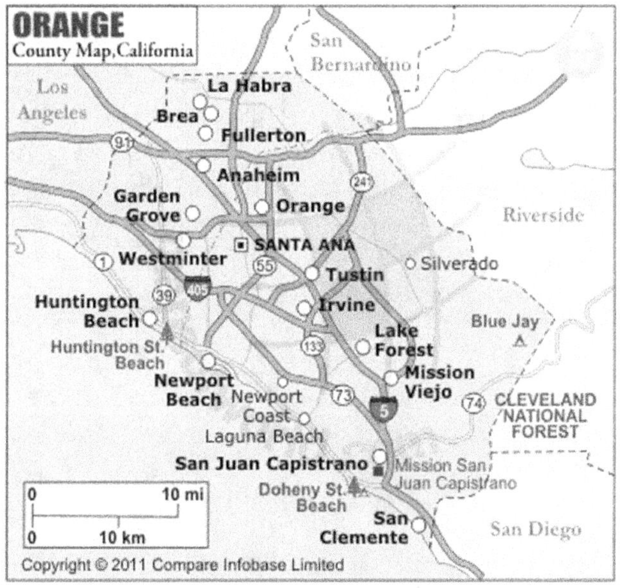

Orange County Map

Although Spain claimed California for more than 200 years, it was not until 1769 that the first efforts were made to colonize the area.

Under Spanish rule, all lands were considered property of the King. A few retired soldiers were granted grazing permits. One of the first was Manuel Nieto, who in 1784 was allowed to occupy all the land between the Santa Ana and the San Gabriel Rivers.

There were 219 mining claims filed in Orange County during the last 30 years. All of the claims were filed under a 142-year-old federal law that still lets citizens search for minerals on public land.

Most all gold discoveries have been in the Santa Ana Mountains, where claims bear such names as Shooting Star, Snake Bite and Y Knott.

Orange County 49er's, Inc. claims to have more than 200 active members and owns 11 mining claims totaling hundreds of acres. The group holds monthly meetings and gold seekers might check them out.

Placer County

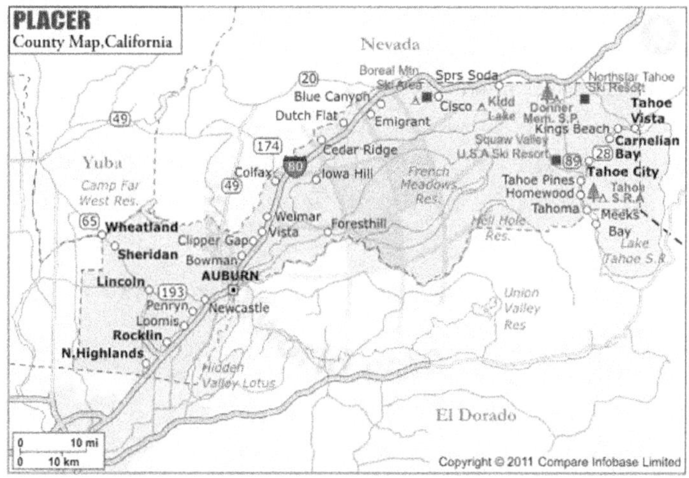

Placer County Map

Gold was found in Placer County in 1848 by Claude Chana, a friend of James Marshall, who discovered gold at Coloma earlier the same year.

Three years after gold was found at Coloma, Placer County was formed from portions of Sutter and Yuba counties. Auburn was the county seat.

Loomis and Newcastle began as mining towns but soon became more famous as fruit growing area. Forest Hill was a lively gold mining town but gradually timber became its mainstay.

Colfax began as a railroad construction camp. In 1865 gold was discovered at the Rising Sun, Montana and Nellie-Meda mines.

In 1850, Forest Hill was a booming gold camp and the site of the famous Jenny Lind mine. At Dutch Flat, 20 miles east of Auburn, German miner Joseph Dorenback and his countrymen began mining in 1851. One nugget alone was worth $5,000.

A favorite place for gold seekers is the Auburn State Recreation Area. It is a public area so mining claims cannot be filed and is open to gold panners.

Plumas County

Plumas County Map

In 1850, the famous African-American mountain man James Beckwourth discovered the lowest pass across the Sierra Nevada. The following year, he navigated a wagon trail for California bound emigrants through Plumas County.

The county gets its name from the Spanish words for the Feather River (*Rio de las Plumas*) which flows through the county. Plumas County was formed in 1854, carved from the eastern portion of Butte County.

In one Plumas County gold mining story, miners trekked up a mountain to get the lay of the land and figure out the best sites for possible gold deposits.

As they climbed the mountain, they found a huge quartz vein exposed on the mountain's slope. They called it the Eureka Lode by the original nine discoverers.

More than three-fourths of Plumas County's 2,618 square miles is National Forest Land.

Of the approximately 4,582,000 ounces of gold produced in Plumas County from 1855 to 1959, more than half came from Tertiary gravel placer mines.

The Gopher Hill, Nelson Point, Sawpit Flat and Upper Spanish Creek mines were in alluvial gravels. Gold was also mined at Green Mountain mine and in the Plumas-Eureka mine.

At Rich Bar on Indian Creek, a tributary of the Feather River, rich placers have been found.

Riverside County

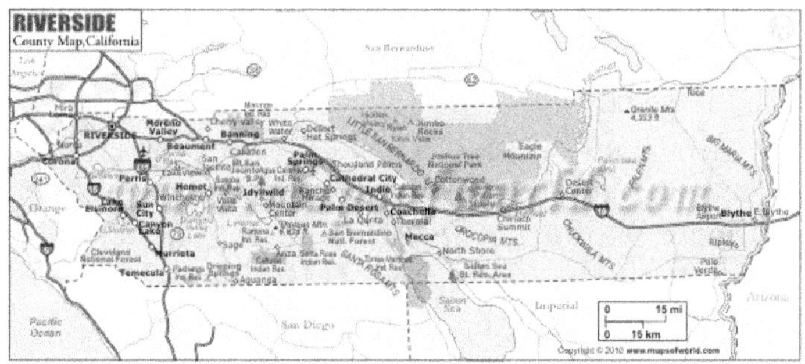

Riverside County Map

By the late 1880s and early 1890s, there was a lot of contention between the towns of Riverside and San Bernardino counties.

San Bernardino was largely Democratic in nature. It allowed saloons and had a hot-bed of secessionist sympathy during the Civil War.

Riverside was temperance minded, allowing few if any saloons and voted Republican.

Both towns were competing for settlers in an area where towns were languishing or dying because of a lack of inhabitants. Charges were flung that claimed unfair use of tax monies to the benefit of San Bernardino.

Several people from Riverside decided to investigate the possibility of a new county. They were joined by residents of Temecula and San Jacinto valleys and the desert region. All were tired of living so far from their county seats.

Riverside County was formed in 1893 by carving out a small portion of San Bernardino County and a larger portion of San Diego County.

Gold deposits are distributed rather widely throughout Riverside County. The Ida Leona mine is located six miles west of Perris. Records indicate there was gold mining in the area as early 1861.

At one time, the top-producing gold mine in Southern California operated in Perris. There are four miles of tunnels under Highway 74. Today, virtually all buildings and equipment are gone, although the mine tailings remain.

The United States Geological Service lists numerous mines registered in Riverside County. It is assumed that the mines are on private property.

Sacramento County

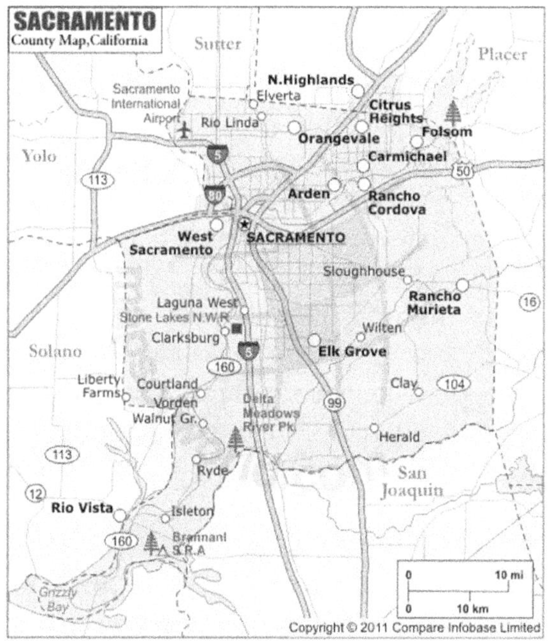

Sacramento County Map

John Augustus Sutter established the town of Sacramento at the confluence of the Sacramento and American rivers. Sacramento is the oldest incorporated city in California.

Sutter was granted 44,000 acres by Mexican Governor Juan Bautista Alvarado.

Alvarado needed to establish a presence in Sacramento and realized that Sutter's ambitions would allow him to secure the big valley without committing troops there.

In January 1850, a major flood ravaged the ground on which the city of Sacramento stood. The American and the Sacramento rivers crested simultaneously and the Embarcadero washed away in the flood.

Hardin Bigelow, the city's first elected mayor, advocated building the first levees and dams to guard Sacramento from future floods.

Bigelow remained in office for seven months before succumbing to cholera.

In 1853, a mammoth project was proposed to raise the new-born city above the flood level. This proposal wasn't fully accepted. It took another flood which devastated the area in 1862 to open the eyes of officials.

Within a few years, thousands of cubic yards of earth were brought in by wagons to raise the level of the streets. The original level can still be seen under the board walks in Old Sacramento.

The center of the commercial district of Sacramento City gradually moved eastward and the city on Sutter's Embarcadero became one of the worst skid row areas west of Chicago.

Reformers, ministers, politicians and others railed against the degraded community, but little was done to change the slum's basic condition.

A strain developed between John Sutter, Sr. and John Sutter, Jr. The son soon became ill and rarely left the family residence at "Hock Farm", located on the Feather River.

His illness continued and Sutter, Jr., became tired of his responsibilities. He wanted to sell his holdings, but figured they were too vast to sell. Some Sacramento businessmen, including the conniving Sam Brannan, heard about Sutter's, Jr.'s desire to sell.

The businessmen drew up a contract and urged young Sutter to sign and get out of California and go where the climate was more suitable to his condition.

Sutter, Jr., read the terms, and was not happy with them. Under pressure from Brannan and the other businessmen, he reluctantly signed the agreement.

Young Sutter moved to Acapulco, Mexico where he married Carmen Rivas. They had a son, John Sutter III. During this time, he was involved in court cases over the sale of his property to Brannan and the lack of payment for the property.

These court cases did not benefit Sutter, Jr., except to release him from the burden of caring for the estate.

Sacramento County produced more than six million ounces of placer gold and 5,000 ounces of lode gold between the years 1880 and 1959.

Gold seekers should try their luck along the Cosumnes River, where stream and terrace gravels contain gold.

There is an online report that a few companies have developed a side trade in culling the precious metals from the building materials they sell. The processes are very secretive about reclaiming gold from the gravel they sell.

One person with the California Geological Survey said, “It’s such a secretive thing that I don’t think anyone quite knows when it got started.”

The ancient riverbed near Rancho Cordova has been mined for aggregate at least since the turn of the 20th century.

There are historic mounds of gravel in the land south of the American River. The mounts in Folsom are referred to as the “Folsom Potatoes”.

San Benito County

Map of San Benito County

San Benito County, named for Saint Benjamin, was created from a portion of Monterey County, with certain additions coming from Merced and Fresno counties.

The policy of establishing mission in California continued after Father Junipero Serra's death. Friar Danti and Lieutenant Sal and a party left Monterey to explore the San Benito Valley.

Mission San Juan Bautista (St. John the Baptist) opened.

The church once had a chime of nine very fine-toned bells, cast in Peru, of which only one is now remaining.

One of more unfortunate tales out of San Benito County involves the toxic New Idria mine. The New Idria Mercury Mine extracted mercury from the abundant cinnabar deposits in the rock formations.

The discovery of mercury ore at New Idria came soon after the discovery of gold in the Sierra foothills. This became very important as mercury was used in extracting gold from ore.

Before the New Idria and New Almaden Quicksilver mines, the mercury came almost exclusively from Europe.

The New Idria Mining District is known for its abundance of rare minerals such as benitoite. Benitoite, the State gemstone, is the collector/specialty stone for which the State is best known.

San Benito County is the only source of this fine, blue colored gem. The area also is home to serpentinite rock, which is used in producing short-fiber asbestos.

San Bernardino County

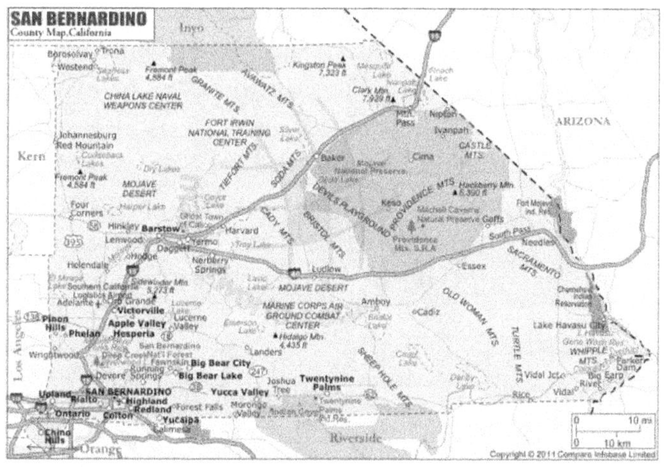

San Bernardino County Map

When the State legislature met in 1850 to divide the state into 27 counties, the area that would become San Bernardino County was a part of what is now San Diego County.

In 1851, Mormon leader Brigham Young gave permission to some of his followers to found a Mormon colony in Southern California. Apostles Amasa Lyman and Charles Rich led a party of 500 men, women and children in 150 wagons from Utah to California.

They arrived at what today is called Devore in the El Cajon Pass in early June. In February, they purchased the San Bernardino Rancho from Don Antonio Maria Lugo, a wealthy Los Angeles land owner.

The San Bernardino Rancho covered 35,509 acres in the San Bernardino and Yucaipa Valley. It was granted to Lugo by Mexican Governor Juan Bautista Alvarado, Lugo's grandnephew.

As a Mormon settlement, San Bernardino lasted only five years. Brigham Young decided to call all his colonists back home to Utah.

In the 1880s, gold was found in the Bear and Holcomb Valleys of the San Bernardino Mountains. This opened up a surge in mining development in the mountains and high desert that still goes on today.

Even though the county has had its acreage cut two or more times since its creation, it remains the largest county in the United States today.

The Clipper Mountains, site of the lost Dutch Oven Mine.

The Lost Dutch Oven Mine is one of the most famous lost mines in California. The mine is located in San Bernardino County. The story relates that Tom Schofield was working for the Santa Fe Railroad at the Danby watering station.

The Danby station's water came from what is known as Bonanza Spring, located in the Clipper Mountains. Schofield manned the Danby Station.

The 42-year-old Schofield traveled on foot to check on Bonanza Spring. One day, he noticed what appeared to be a long-neglected trail leading off to the side of the mountain.

According to one version of the story, Schofield came upon an abandoned miner's camp. He continued up a steep bank and scaled the edge of a narrow shale wall.

Schofield found a mine shaft of some depth, with sides boarded up by old railroad ties. He felt that the tailing pile might contain rich ore. As it was late in the afternoon, he decided to stay the night at the small miner's camp.

When he arose the next morning, he accidentally kicked the lid off of a Dutch oven near the fire pit. Gold ore spilled from the old Dutch oven.

Schofield gathered up as much of the ore as he could carry and headed back down the mountain to his Danby station.

In another version of the Dutch oven story, Schofield hike the trail and came upon an abandoned stone house. He continued hiking for what he estimated to be nine more miles when he came upon a spring.

Schofield followed the trail from the spring over a hill and came up rock or boulder he said was as big as a house. The boulder was split in two and the trail continued through the split.

Beyond this split rock he came upon an old Spanish camp. Beyond that was a high shelf, surrounded by high walls. The only way in or out of the little flat was through the split rock.

He found an old mine shaft, in which lay the skeletons of seven burros. In this story, too, he tripped over a Dutch oven filled with gold ore.

Still a third version of this tale has Schofield hiking the abandoned trail, passing through the split boulder and arriving at a wood cabin with a hitching post.

In front of the hitching post lay the carcasses of several dead burros. In the cabin were the skeletons of three or four humans.

Also in the cabin was a Dutch oven filled with gold ore.

Tom Schofield had the ore had carried away from the legendary sites and the results showed a rich gold content.

For just the nuggets and ore he was able to carry with him, Schofield netted over $200,000.

After spending his newfound money on gambling, liquor and women, Schofield returned to the Clipper Mountains. He searched and searched for the trail that led to the Dutch Oven Mine.

In the 1930s and into the 1940s, when he was in his 80s and early 90s, Schofield still wandered around the Danby station and the Clipper Mountains in search of the Lost Dutch Oven Mine.

The Clipper Mountains are located south of Interstate 40 and the Clipper Valley between the freeway and National Old Trails Highway, near Essex.

There is no record of the Lost Dutch Oven Mine having been found again.

San Bernardino County is the largest county in the United States. It has many scattered mine throughout its desert and mountain ranges.

In the Stedman district, seven miles south of Ludlow, is the Bagdad Mine. Thirty-six miles southwest of Needles in the Turtle Mountains at Carson Wells is the Lost Arch Mine.

San Diego County

San Diego County Map

San Diego County is said to host a trove of hidden treasures.

One is a particularly enchanting story about former slave Fred Coleman, who discovered gold in Julian. History reports that several black pioneers settled in the Julian area of San Diego County.

Fred lived near the base of Volcan Mountain. He and his Native American wife, Maria, had 11 children. Coleman worked as a cowboy on a ranch herding cattle.

While herding cattle in the Spencer Valley area, Coleman stopped alongside a creek to let his horse drink. He saw a glimmer in the creek.

Using the skillet he carried in his saddle bags, Fred began panning for gold.

The San Diego Union reported Coleman's find and it wasn't long before Julian was swarming with prospectors.

Total gold production of gold in San Diego County in the years 1869-1959 was about 219,800 ounces, of which very little was placer mining. Five miles south of Julian, in the vicinity of Banner, some lode mines exist.

In the Ramona District the Spaulding Mine is located. It was a lode gold mine.

It is said that in the flats below the Little Three Mine gold seekers may find placer deposits.

San Francisco County

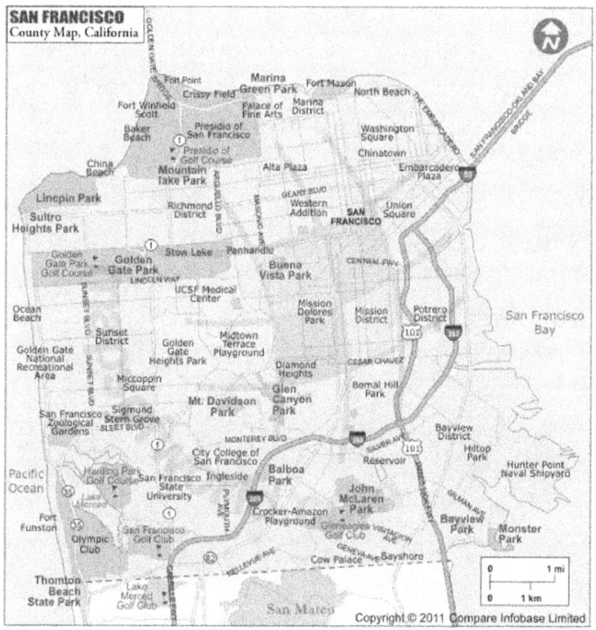

San Francisco County Map

In 1579, Sir Francis Drake, known as much for looting Spanish galleons as for exploring, sailed past the entrance to what is now San Francisco Bay.

Drake named a stretch of Marin "Nova Albion" and sailed away.

Then, the Spaniard Gaspar de Portola, founded the Presidio Army Base.

Just before the history of the 49ers and their gold discovery began, the United States made one of its luckiest purchases. A small outpost of wooden shacks, called Yerba Buena, founded by Sam Brannan, became an official part of the United States.

In less than a year, 50,000 people poured into San Francisco (renamed from Yerba Buena) seeking the newly announced gold in the Sierra Nevada.

Just as San Francisco was settling down from the excitement of the Gold Rush, it suffered a jolt from the sleeping San Andreas Fault in the form of a 7.7 to 7.9 earthquake.

San Francisco thrives today as the "Paris of the West".

San Joaquin County

San Joaquin County Map

Lieutenant Gabriel Moraga led an expedition into the lower great California Central Valley. He gave the name San Joaquin (meaning Joachim which has religious significance) to the San Joaquin River.

Gold production has been sporadic in San Joaquin County. Most of it has come from the

Quaternary placers along the Mokelumne River between the towns of Clements and Comanche and along the Calaveras River near Bellota, Linden and Jenny Lind. From 1918 to 1920, there was a brief spurt of activity.

Numerous gravel deposits have been recorded along the Calaveras River containing rich placer gold.

San Luis Obispo County

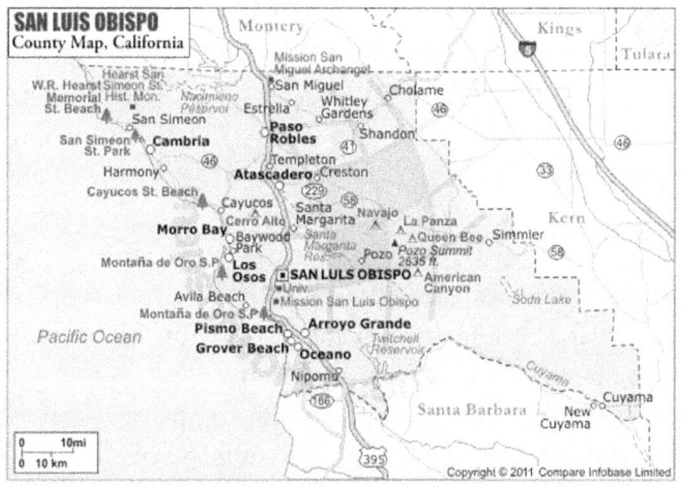

San Luis Obispo County Map

In 1769, Gaspar de Portola traveled through San Luis Obispo County on his way to rediscover the Bay of Monterey. His diarist, Padre Juan Crespi, recorded the name given the area as *llano de los Osos*, or the level of the bears (Bear Plain).

Father Junipero Serra, who founded a second mission, San Carlos Borremeo, in Monterey, remembered the Valley of the Bears when supplies dwindled at his four missisons.

He sent a hunting expedition to bring back food in 1872. More than 25 mules loads of dried bear meat and seed was sent north to relieve the missions.

It was then that Father Serra determined San Luis Obispo would be a good site for his fifth mission.

An interesting institution is California Polytechnic University established in 1901. Its first incoming class was 20 students. It grew steadily until 1910s when World War 1 led to drops in enrollment.

In 1901, Cal Poly opened as a coeducational school with 40 new male students and 12 new female students. In 1930, Cal Poly banned females from the school until 1956. Now female students comprise 46 percent of enrollment.

Throughout San Luis Obispo County gold has been found and mined. It is mostly in the "flour" variety.

Don't fret, even a pan full of color is worth some real dollars. Flour gold that once was nice for a "golden show" and fun to look at but worth only 50 cents now has value.

Only three locations in the county have produced sizeable nuggets. West of Paso Robles, in the mountain country. Most of the property is private. Nuggets have been found on San Luis Obispo cattle ranches.

On the Jack Ranch, now owned by the Hearst Corporation, there is a butte behind the headquarters known as Gold Hill. The Mission Padres of San Miguel Mission and the Mission Indians mined gold there around 1805.

Gold has also been found in the Castle Mountains.

San Mateo County

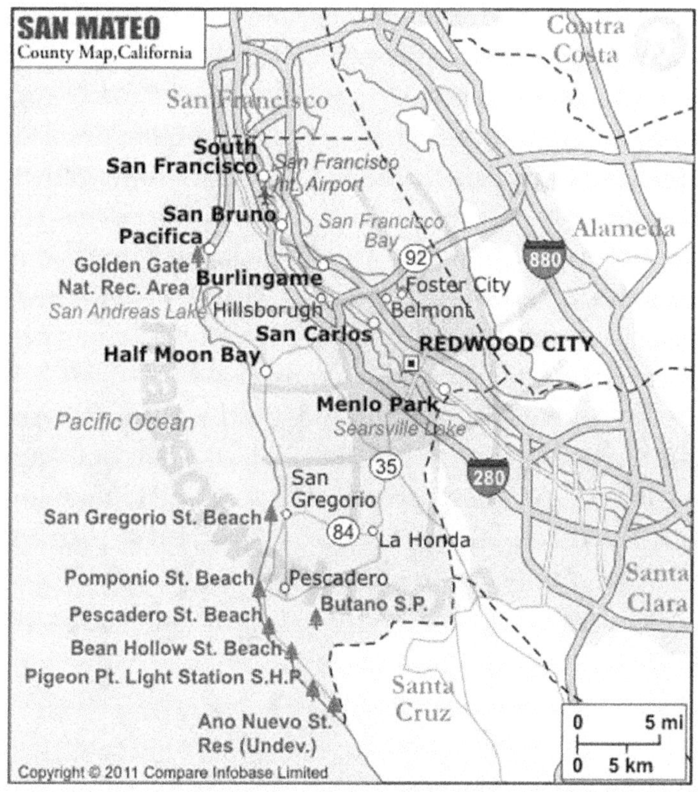

San Mateo County Map

San Mateo County was formed in 1856. It was one of the state's original 18 counties. Until 1856, San Francisco's city limits extended west to Divisadero and Castro Street.

In response to the lawlessness and vigilantism that escalated between 1855 and 1856, California government officials decided to divide San Francisco County.

A straight line was drawn across the tip of the San Francisco Peninsula just north of San Bruno Mountain. Everything south of the line became the new San Mateo County.

San Mateo County bears the Spanish name for Saint Matthew. Until 1850, the name appeared as San Matheo.

San Mateo County is the 13th largest county in California. Its population is 712,400. Of these people, approximately 63,500 live in the unincorporated area of the County.

It is considered one of most ethnically diverse communities in the nation: 49.8 percent are Caucasion, 21.8 percent are Hispanic, 21 paercent Asian-Pacific Islander, 3.3 percent African American, and 4.1 percent are listed as other.

No data was found on gold panning opportunities.

Santa Barbara County

When explorer Sebastian Viscaino sailed into the channel of Santa Barbara in 1602, he called in Santa Barbara in memory of Saint Barbara, virgin and martyr.

In 1822, the citizens of Santa Barbara swore allegiance to the Empire of Mexico, ending Spanish rule in California.

The present county of Ventura was originally included within Santa Barbara County.

Santa Barbara County had its own brief flurry of a gold rush when gold was found in the Santa Ynez River, and later at Point Sal and Point Pedernales.

Mariano Lopez was the majordomo of Dr. Richard S. Den's Rancho San Marcos. While returning from mass at Santa Inez Mission, Lopoez paused to water his horse.

A yellow glint in the ripples of the river caught his eye. The reminded him of stories told by his father about Mission padres working a secret gold mine farther up the canyon.

This mine was said to be "...thirty miles by mule trail north of Santa Barbara".

He took his find to a Santa Barbara druggist named Benigno Gutierrez. Gutierrez tested the ore with nitric and hydrochloric acid and did a malleability test. He found that each tiny grin could be stamped as thin as a butterfly's wing.

Lopez attempted to keep his find secret but soon San Marcos Pass was thronged with gold seekers.

In 1889, prospectors discovered that the beach sands at Point Sal and Point Pedernales yielded gold worth $6 for every ton of sand worked. Two mining companies set up operations there.

Santa Clara County

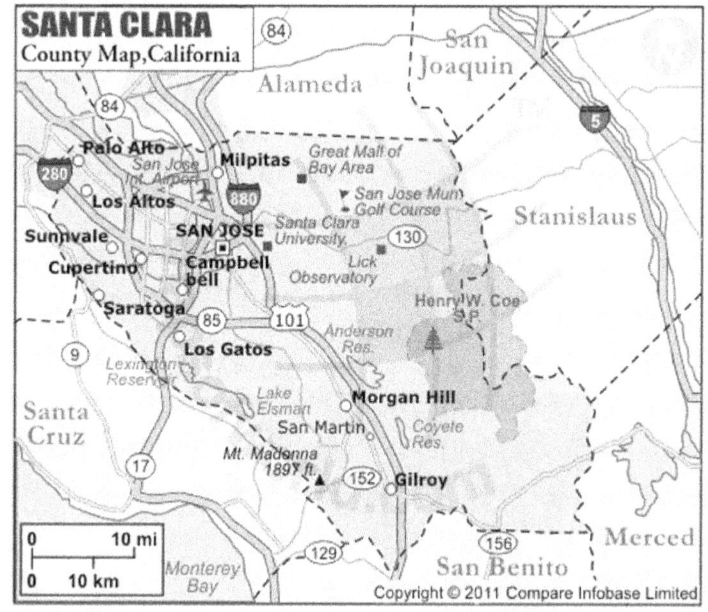

Santa Clara County Map

Santa Clara Valley was created by the sudden growth of the Santa Cruz Mountains and the Diablo Mountain Range during the Cenozoic era.

This was a period of intense mountain building in California. The folding and thrusting of the earth's crust, combined with active volcanism, gave shape to the present state of California.

San Jose was California's first town. In 1777, on orders from the Spanish viceroy of Mexico, five *pobladores (*settlers*)* with their families, and one cowboy, were detailed to found the Pueblo de San Jose de Guadalupe, named in honor of Saint Joseph.

San Jose became the first capital of the State of California.

Mexican settler Antonio Sunol discovered ore deposits in Santa Clara County in the 1820s. It was identified as quicksilver.

New Almaden attracted a world-wide interest during the Gold Rush, since mercury was the primary reduction agent of gold and silver.

Santa Cruz County

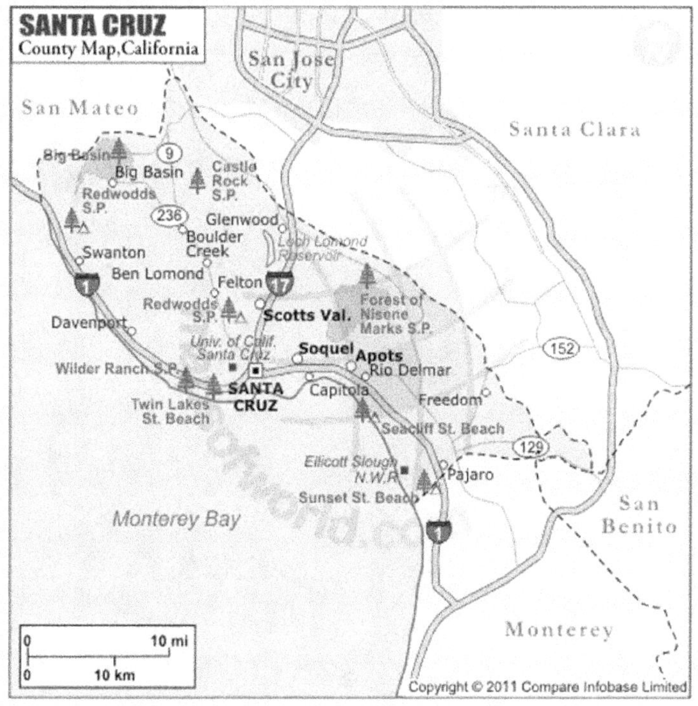

Santa Cruz County Map

When established in 1850 as one of the original counties in California, it was given the name of "Branciforte" after the Spanish pueblo founded there in 1797. Branciforte Creek still bears that name.

Gold occurs in Santa Cruz County in auriferous black sand deposits, in placer deposits and in a number of creeks and gulches on the sides of Ben Lomond Mountain.

The principal placers were on Waddell Creek, Majors Creek and Gold Gulch.

Shasta County

Shasta County Map

Map showing Clear Creek, once called Horsetown.

The first known gold discovered in Shasta County was made by Pierson B. Reading in 1848. Reading found the gold on a bar in Clear Creek. He washed out fifty-two ounces of gold daily.

A gold camp grew up on a flat adjoining the bar. It was first called “Clear Creek Diggings”. By October 1849, more than 300 miners congregated at Clear Creek Diggings.

One of these prospectors, who arrived in camp with one pack horse, settled there permanently and later built a hotel. The story is that the name of Clear Creek Diggings was changed to "One Horse Town".

Later, it boasted 3,000 residents, with two hotels, stores, sops, a Catholic Church, a newspaper (the Northern Argus) and fourteen saloons.

The site of Reading's Bar and One Horse Town are located east of the Clear Creek Bridge seven miles west of State Route 273 on Clear Creek Road.

One Horse Town was destroyed by fire in 1868 and the site has been thoroughly

In 1853, a newspaper reported that there wasn't a river, creek, gulch or ravine that didn't contain gold.

Mining began in a haphazard way, with shovels, picks, pans, and even knives and spoons.

Gold dominated the mineral economy of Shasta County until 1897 when copper became king.

A two-pound gold nugget was found by Waldo Elmore on his claim in the Flat Creek Mining District in 1890s. In 1878, a 13 ounce crystallized chunk of gold was taken from the Mad Mule Mine and exhibited in the 1878 Paris Exposition.

In 1912, a 19 1/2 ounce nugget was taken in Mad Mule Canyon.

In 1870, three miners found a 184.5 ounce gold nugget on Spring Creek a short distance below the falls near the Iron Mountain Railway Crossing.

Sierra County

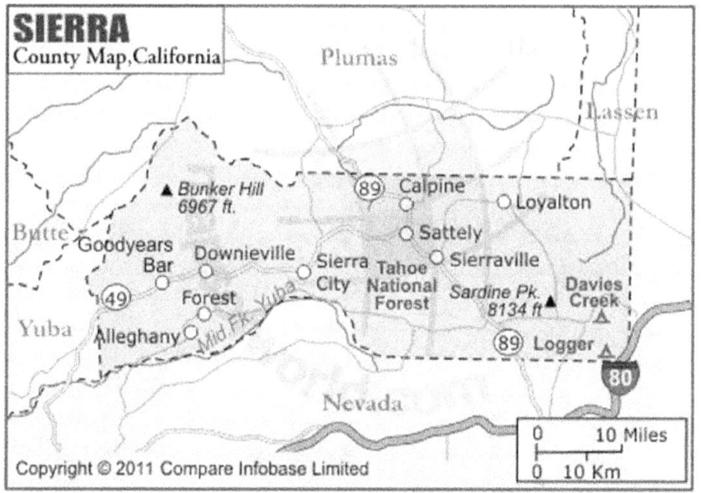

Sierra County Map

Sierra County divided by the Pacific Crest. Both the east and the west have rich histories.

The county was once the home to both the Maidu and the Washoe Indians.

When gold was discovered there, 16,000 miners rushed into the area. Dozens of gold camp communities with such colorful names as Brandy City, Poker Flat, Poverty Hill and Whiskey Diggins thrived.

The Original Sixteen to One Mine in the little hamlet of Alleghany bases its business model on specimen gold. The work is all done by hand and there is no toxic waste.

Minnesota Flat and Chip's Flat had many high-yielding gold mines. Mines were located between Downieville and the Middle Fork of the Yuba River.

Among the mines located in Sierra County were the Empire Mine, the Plumbago Mine, the Sixteen to One, the Kate Hardy, German Bar, the Ruby, the Oriflame, the Delhi, Idaho, Maryland, Brunswick, giant King and the Sadie D.

A specimen gold find at the Sixteen to One Mine in Alleghany.

Downieville is the county seat of Sierra County and is located on Highway 49 at the fork of the North Yuba and Downie Rivers.

Alleghany developed into a town from the consolidation of several mining locations in the early 1850s. The Sixteen to One Mine still operates.

One gold prospector comments that he has personally dredged Kanaka Creek with a 3" and 5" inch dredge below the Kenton Mine. "This is one of the richest creeks in the Mother Lode as far as I'm concerned."

Check the BLM offices to get even more prospecting sites in this rich county.

Siskiyou County

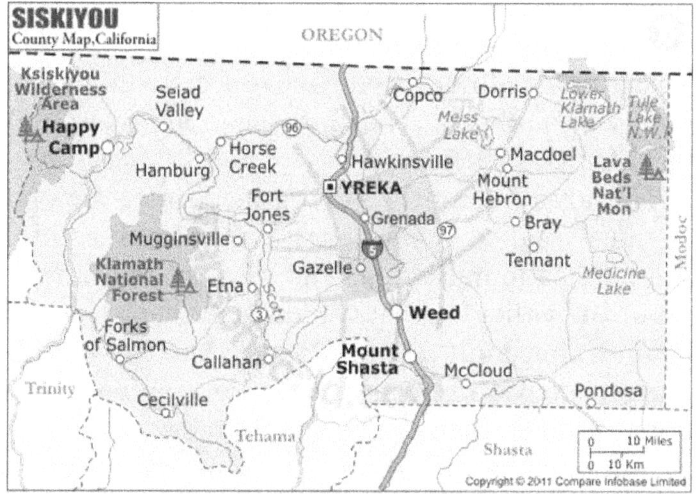

A map of Siskiyou County

Siskiyou County lies at the heart of the famous Northern Mines. The county has more than 370 gold mines in its history, dating back to 1850.

The county is graced with majestic granite peaks and rocky streams that incite gold miners to seek the gold in mountain sides and the rushing waters.

In 1851, a mule-train packer named Abraham Thompson saw flakes of gold among the grass roots that his mules were chomping near Black Gulch.

Word got out and soon after, 2,000 miners were in the area hoping to strike it rich. They erected tents and shanties, and a boomtown arose.

It was called by several names until eventually, the name Yreka was applied to the town and it exists as such today. It's estimated that millions of dollars have been mined from the area.

One group of prospector found gold on the South Fork of the Salmon River above Cecilville in 1849. More was found on the flats near a ravine called Black Gulch in 1851.

The area currently known as Shasta City was previously called Strawberry Valley because of the wild berries found there. The town at the northern end of the valley was first named "Wheelocks" after the man that built a trading post there. It was then changed to Ottiitiewa, the Indian name for the Scott Valley branch of the Shasta tribe.

It finally became Fort Jones in 1860 after the U.S. Army build a fort there.

The county is said to contain large Platinum Group metals as well as gold.

Good areas to prospect for gold include along several creeks, including Cottonwood, Deadwood, Dillon, Elk, Horse, Humbug and Indian creeks.

The Klamath River has gold deposits along its entire length in Siskiyou County.

The Klamath River contains placer gold along its entire course. Some of the best locations are where creeks come into the river.

Solano County

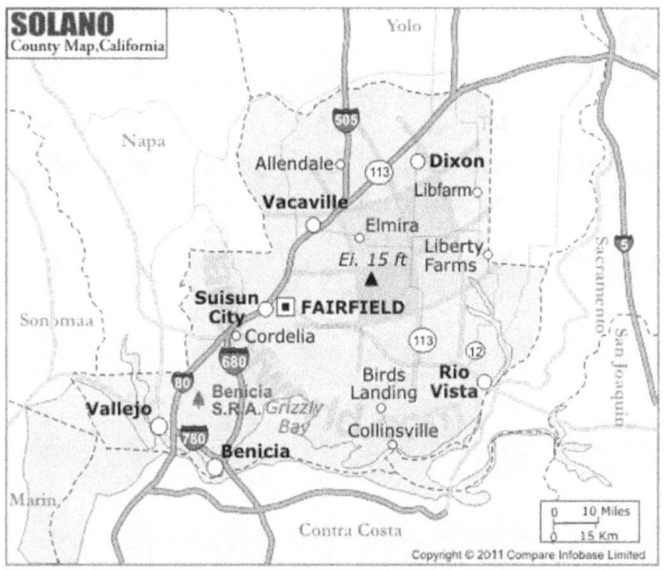

Solano County Map

Artifacts of stone-age people have been found in Green Valley dating back to 2,000 B.C.E.

At the request of General Mariano Guadalupe Vallejo in 1850 at the time California's counties were designated, the area was named Solano, after an Indian Chief. Chief Solano at one time led the tribes between the Petaluma River and the Sacramento River.

Infected with gold fever, Vallejo residents Christian Mangold and George Ashley prospected around Green Valley for a year. In late 1886, they discovered traces of gold in the valley. They began tracking the source.

They purchased the sixteen-acre property. Assays later showed that the entire mountain was worth $5 a ton. About one-third ounce of gold was being extracted from each ton of ore.

Gold was also found in Putah Creek in Vacaville in the 1930s. Berryessa Dam now covers the area where the gold was found.

Sonoma County

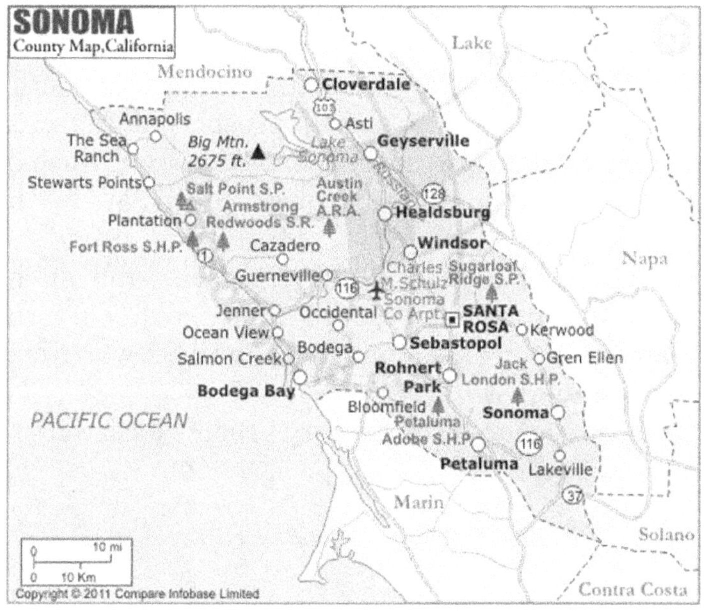

Sonoma County Map

This is area was first occupied by Russians who established a foothold by building Fort Ross on the Sonoma Coast in 1812. The fort was sold to John Sutter in 1841.

Sonoma was one of California's original counties. The rapidly growing communities of Petaluma, Santa Rosa and Healdsburg began vying with Sonoma to have the county seat moved to their towns.

There is a story that Joseph Hooker, of Sonoma, introduced a bill that resulted in Santa Rosa being confirmed as the County Seat. It is said that several Santa Rosans decided to take immediate action and rode down the Sonoma Valley, took the county seals and records and brought them back to Santa Rosa.

A Sonoma County woman, armed only with a milk pan and a fire shovel prospected the creek near her home for several months. Her husband laughed at her and she was joked at by her neighbors.

She found a little patch of black sand on her claim and it yielded $3 in flake gold. On other occasions she washed out more than $2 worth with a few minutes work.

Gold seekers should try their luck on the Russian River.

Stanislaus County

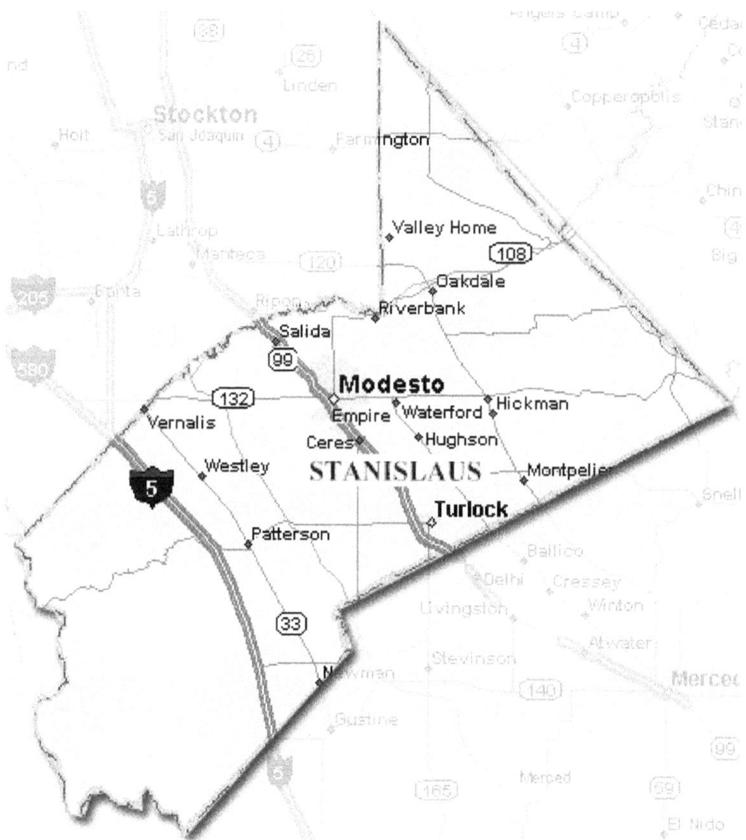

Stanislaus County Map

Stanislaus County was created in 1854 by taking a portion of Tuolumne County. The word Stanislaus is a corruption of Estanislao, the baptismal name of a mission-educated renegade Indian chief.

Estanislao led a band of Indians in a series of battles against Mexican troops. He was finally defeated by General Mariano G. Vallejo in 1826.

In the early 1900s, large-scale dredging of Quaternary gravels began along the Tuolumne River and La Grange and Waterford. Most of the gold produced from 1932 to 1959 came from this area.

Sutter County

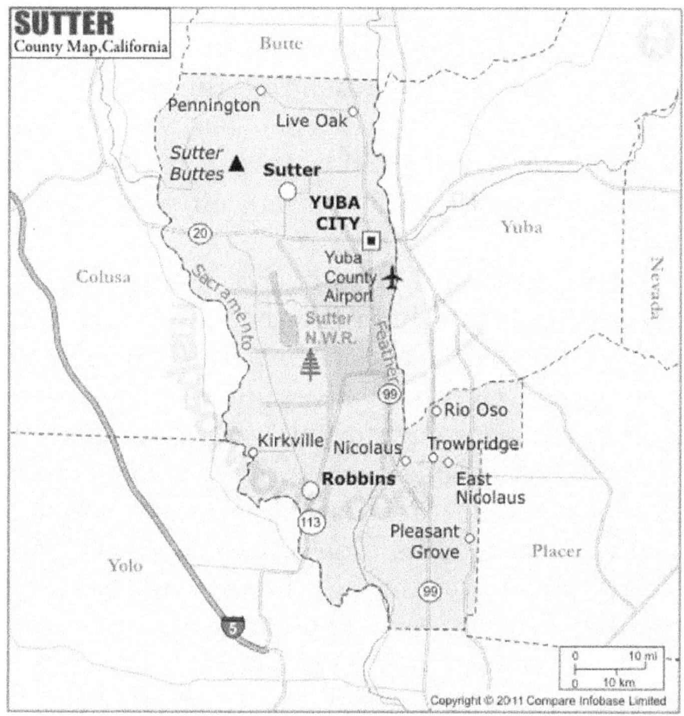

Sutter County Map

John Sutter owned the lumber mill where James Marshall discovered gold at Coloma in 1848. It was eventually, the flood of prospectors to California that ended empire as squatters took over his lands.

Like his European experiences, Sutter failed just as badly at his American business ventures. He was said to be something of a linguist, and became fluent in Spanish while traveling the southwest.

Sutter found his way to Hawaii by way of a Hudson's Bay Company ship. While there, he convinced an American merchant to let him have a ship for a trading expedition to California.

He traveled to California by way of Sitka, Alaska, taking the trouble to gather letters from British, American, and Russian officials along the way.

Sutter used the letters he had collected to convince Governor Juan Bautista Alvarado that he would be a valuable man to have in California.

He asked Governor Alvarado for land so could settle in the Sacramento Valley. His rancho would become a buffer zone against the Indians as well as against the Americans coming over the mountains. Alvarado granted him nine square leagues of land.

Sutter had brought with him from Hawaii eight "kanaka" laborers, and two of their wives, as well as three Anglos. He established a fort where the city of Sacramento is today.

From these headquarters, Sutter took possession of a 50,000-acre tract of land in the Sacramento River Valley. He became a Mexican citizen and fully intended to carve out a princely empire.

Wearing a general's uniform, which he favored, Sutter called his establishment New Helvetia (New Switzerland) and maintained an army at the fort.

John Sutter put everyone to work, Hawaiians, Americans, Indians, Californios, as he developed his empire. He acquired an additional two leagues of land from later Governor Manuel Micheltorena, and claimed a lot more simply because no one else had.

He acquired cattle, and dealt in beaver skins, lumber, and agricultural products. Sutter's Fort was on the direct east-west route and became a convenient stopping place for travelers.

Sutter had the bad fortune, however, of being located in the exact spot where gold was discovered in large quantities. He eventually lost everything he had to the gold seekers swarming into California and across his land.

Several thousand squatters moved in on the unfortunate Swiss' 11-square-league land grant. Those people who had purchased land from him held title legally, but others settled on land they had not bought.

In August, 1850, some of the squatters' leaders were arrested. This only caused the squatters to band together in an army to free their leaders. In the melee that followed, the mayor and sheriff of Sacramento were shot and killed, and it was evident that law and order would not prevail in Sacramento.

In his old age, Sutter, living in Pennsylvania, petitioned the United States Congress for a pension, but the Supreme Court disallowed his claim.

Sutter County has been slight in mineral production. A few metals, including gold, silver, and quicksilver have been found in the Marysville Buttes.

Tehama County

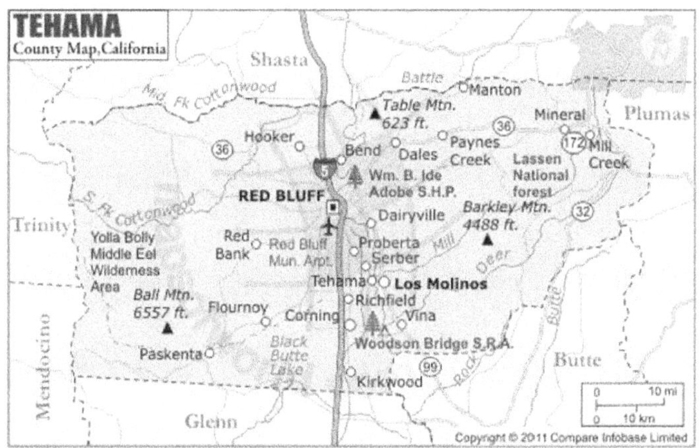

Strangely, nobody seems to know the origin of the word Tehama or what it means. We did find one source that indicates it is of Hawaiian origin and named by employees of Peter Lassen.

There is another story that says an Indian maiden called out to non-Indians crossing a stream, *Te-ha-ma,* meaning shallow. The non-Indians understood and crossed successfully.

For lack of a better meaning, we'll take this one.

A black mark against Tehama County came in 1886 when the town of Red Bluff demanded that Leland Stanford dismiss all of his Chinese workers.

Stanford rebuffed the demand, with a caustic letter of his own: *The Chinaman is entitled to the same just treatment, while in our country, as any other foreigner, or any other citizen."*

Trinity County

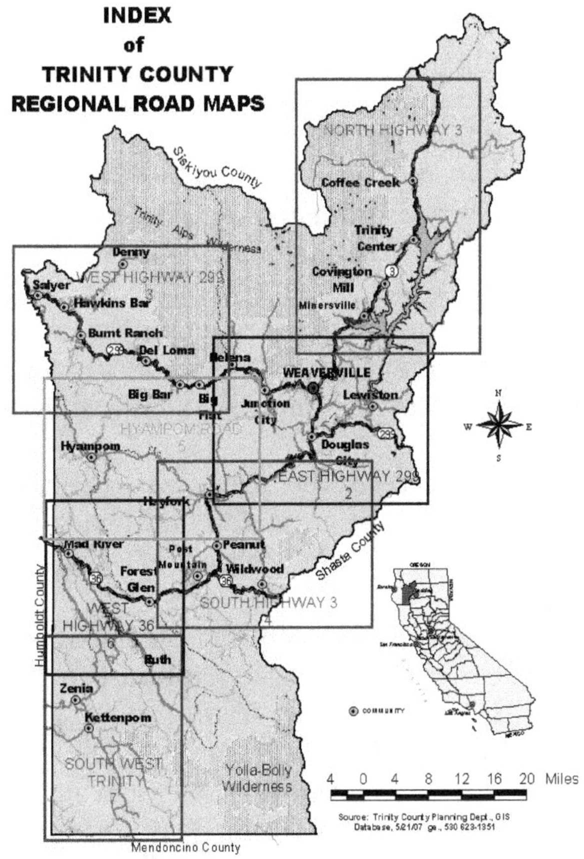

A map of Trinity County

There is an unwritten rule for gold miners. If there is a comfortable place to pan, the gold is not there. This doesn't mean that you can't bring a buck full of dirt, river or stream bottom, carry to that comfort area and do the panning there.

There are places that gold is most likely to be trapped. If the current in some part a stream is slower, it gives the gold a chance to settle there.

Trinity County is located in the lower reaches of the Cascade Mountain range in California, midway between Redding in Shasta County and the Northern Redwood Coast.

Trinity County is roughly the size of Vermont, although if it were flattened out, it might cover an area the size of Texas.

The easy gold pickings were clean out long ago with very low frequency metal detectors.

At one time the streams of Weaverville were rich in gold.

The first settler in the area was Pearson B. Reading. In 1844, he received a Mexican land grant near Redding. He named it Rancho de Buenaventura.

When gold was discovered at Coloma by James Marshall, it caused Reading to explore the Trinity River system. He mined the Trinity near Douglas City, at what is now Reading's Bar.

On his return, he blazed the Shasta-Weaverville Road traveling over the Trinity Mountains and down to the gold rush community of Shasta.

In 1851, Weaverville consisted of one round tent and four log cabins. Two years later a school and a hospital were established. The community was incorporated in 1855.

Productive placer gold locations have been found along the east fork of the Trinity River, especially in the Indian Creek tributary.

Placer gold is also located in the gravels of the Trinity River stream, bench and terrace gravels.

Tulare County

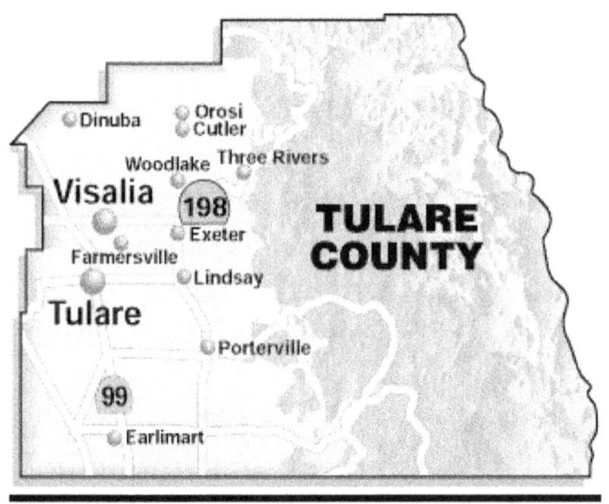

Tulare County Map

More than 60 gold mines are scattered throughout Tulare County. Only those in the White River district where gold was discovered in 1853 have had significant production.

It is estimated that Tulare County produced more than 21,000 ounces of gold since mining began there.

The county has two gold-mining districts. One is the White River District and the other is the Mineral King District. The White River District has played a greater part in Tulare County's gold history than has the Mineral King District.

Some of the mines were created to recover other types of ore, and gold was just a lucky by-product.

The first settlers to the Tulare area were led by a man named John Woods. He built a cabin as a lodge for travelers. A town called Woodsville sprang up in the area of the cabin.

With the Gold Rush in full force, many travelers were heading past Tulare County. The little town of Woodsville burned to the ground in 1850 and almost all of its inhabitants massacred by the Kaweah Indian tribe.

When the Indians swooped down on Woodsville, they slayed several, some say fourteen. Two men jumped into the Kaweah River. Keeping their heads under water, they were able to drift down the river to safety.

Only John Wood reached the cabin and sought refuge behind the stout door. A number of the men had left their rifles in the cabin, and Wood had rifles and ammunition at his disposal.

The Indians, armed only with knives and bows and arrows. The arrows were made of willow and could do little damage to the cabin. Late in the day, the Indians made a final rush and succeeded in reaching the cabin.

The following account has been given of the massacre.

They laid John Wood on the ground and proceeded to cut off his skin. They began at his finger and toes, and then took the skin off his arms and legs, then off his back. Woods endured the treatment in silence.

Tuolumne County

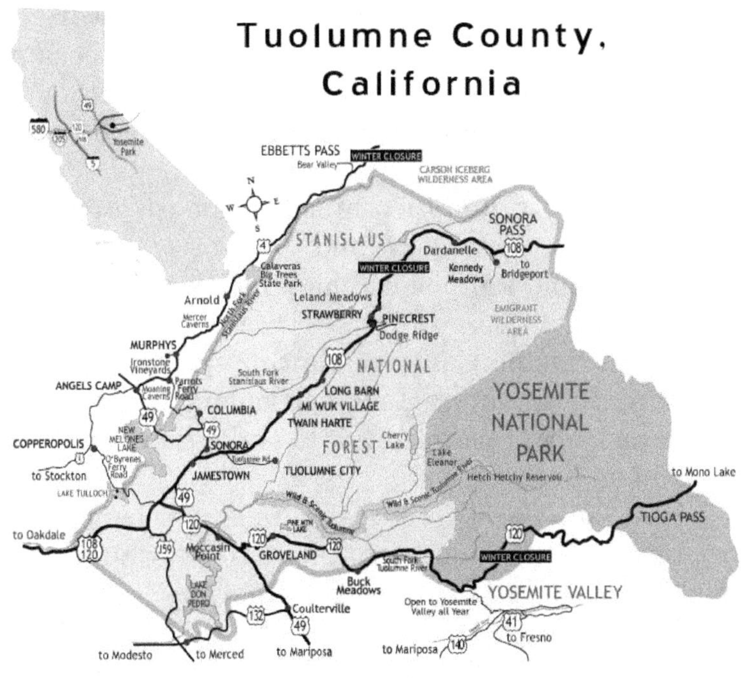

Map of Tuolumne County

Following James Marshall's gold discovery in Coloma in 1848, gold was found in what is now Tuolumne County.

An Oregon prospector named Benjamin Wood led a party that found gold on the banks of a branch of the Tuolumne River. The site was later called Wood's Crossing and Wood's Creek.

Then, Colonel George James from San Francisco started a mining camp above Wood's Crossing. He named it Jamestown, after himself.

Mexican and Chilean prospector began working claims upstream on Wood's Creek that became known as Santiago. They secretly moved further up Wood's Creek in what is today known as Columbia Way, in the northern portion of Sonora.

Tuolumne County foothills became covered with gold miners, gamblers and all sorts of people. Crime became a problem, changing the atmosphere dramatically.

There was no California law or system of courts for settling disputes. Each settlement made up its own rules about claims, how to stake them and how to hold on to them.

In 1850, the Foreign Miners Act became law, requiring all foreigners to pay $20 per month tax for the privilege of mining in California.

Some foreign miners struck back with violence and the gold field became dangerous as robberies and killings became frequent. Vigilante groups formed, punishing many by hanging suspected criminals without legal trials.

Even after the repeal of the Foreign Miners Act, trouble persisted up until 1858.

In 1852, a chunk of gold weighing 45 pounds, worth $8,000, was found near Sonora. The finder had a friend who was far gone with consumption, but who was still trying to work in the mines. The owner of the nugget saw that the miner was fast killing himself.

At that time, such a mass of gold would attract curious people from all around. The nugget owner arranged for the sick miner to take the nugget to the States for exhibition purposes.

Besides the huge nugget, he also took some fine dust, called chispas, some gold bearing quartz, black sand, and other ore. He delivered lectures on mining operations in California.

For a time, the nugget owner heard from his friend regularly then lost track of him. He began to think his friend had been murdered for the nugget.

Then, one day, a letter reached the miner from a banker in New Orleans telling him his friend had died in that city. He had left the big nugget at the bank subject to his order.

The miner wrote to have the nugget melted down. The bank issued him a check a little more than $8,000.

The Forty-Niners are gone but there is still plenty of gold left in Tuolumne County.

The Gold Prospectors Association of America reports a twenty percent increase in membership from last year, to 50,000.

Brandon Johnson, director of operations for the association, said he was in Nome, Alaska, and where he used to see five or six people using dredges on a beach, you now see 18 to 20 of them.

"People are selling their gold to pay the bills," he said.

Ventura County

Ventura County Map

The Southern Pacific Railroad laid tracks through San Buenaventura in 1887. For convenience in printing their timetables, Southern Pacific shortened San Buenaventura to Ventura. The post office followed suit.

It was known that oil existed in Ventura County as far back as the Chumash Indians who first occupied the area. The Chumash used tar to make baskets and canoes waterproof.

A disaster happened in Ventura County in 1928 when the St. Francis Dam collapsed, sending billions of gallons of water crashing through the Santa Clara Valley, killing 385 people and destroying 1,240 homes.

Recreational miners have found gold in Piru Creek in north Ventura County.

Yolo County

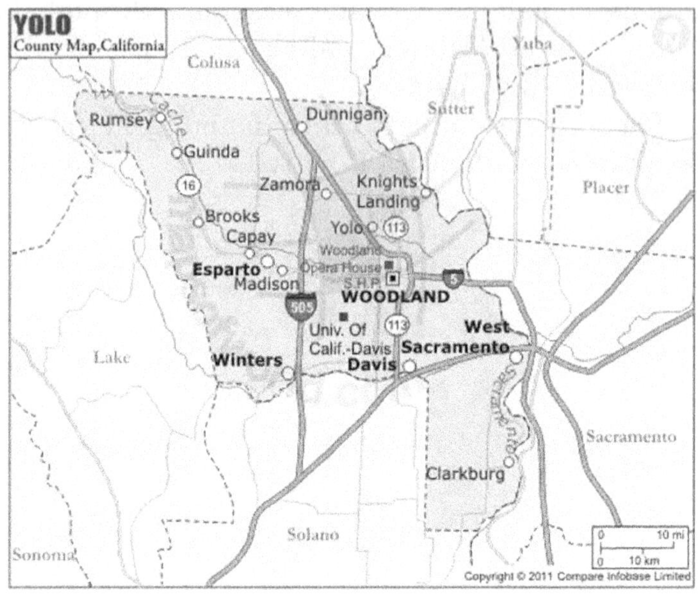

Yolo County Map

Yolo County lies at the center of California. It is located in California's great central valley.

More money has been expended in irrigation enterprises in the last two years than in all of Yolo County's history.

Unlike most counties, Yolo County is said to be out of debt and has the lowest tax rate, with one or two exceptions, of any county in Northern California.

Yolo County is the home of the University of California, located in Davis.

Writer Bo Spiers tells of a gold mining trick old timers used in processing gold ore. The process used mercury to separate the ore from the gold.

In rural areas the amalgamated gold and mercury were often placed on a shovel and heated over a fire, leaving behind the collected gold in the form of nuggets.

A smaller-scale procedure involved cutting a potato in half, scooping out the pulp and filling it with amalgam. The potato was then wired together and placed on a bed of coals. In a couple of hours, the potato could be opened to reveal a small nugget of gold.

Yuba County

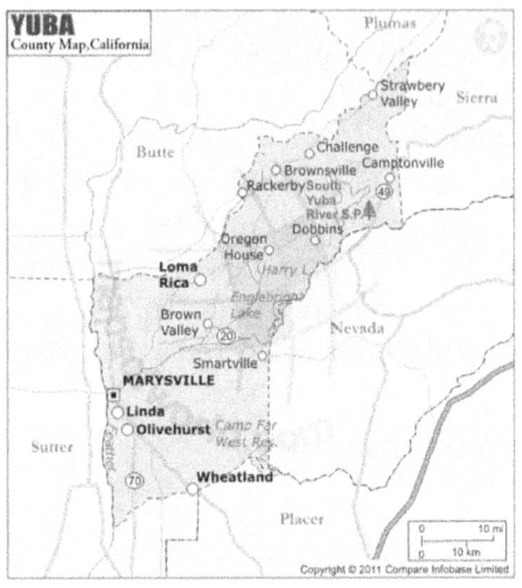

Yuba County Map

Yuba County stood first in the state for many years as a gold producer. It still commands a leading position.

In Yuba County, about seven miles east of Marysville, is the largest gold dredger in the world. It cost about $750,000 and its bucket line digs 120 feet from the surface of the water to 15 feet below the surface of the ground.

The Yuba Goldfields is a valley of 10,000 acres on both sides of the Yuba River. The goldfields are noted for their oddly shaped gravel mountains, ravines, streams and turquoise-colored pools of water.

The goldfields were created during the California Gold Rush. Mining companies moved from the valley floor into the Sierra Nevada foothills, blasting away with their high-pressure jets of water.

It is estimated that 685,000,000 cubic feet of debris was deposited in the Yuba River. The debris ended raised the riverbed by up to 100 feet, causing floods the buried farms east of Marysville.

In 1893, the California Debris Commission began to dredge the Yuba near Marysville to mitigate the damage. The gravel was piled along the river's banks, creating the irregular hills seen today.

The dredgers created more than 200 ponds which are fed by a network of underground rivers. The water in those ponds is usually clear blue, the impurities have been filtered by the gravel.

The towns of Smartsville and Timbuctoo celebrate Pioneer Day on the last Saturday of April.

This annual festival honors the early settlers of the two communities, both original Yuba County Gold Rush towns.

Exhibits of gold panning and blacksmithing are shown during the festival. There are tours of hydraulic mining area, local cemeteries and what life was like in the Gold Rush days.

Meet the Author

Alton Pryor

Alton Pryor has published fifty-plus books since turning 70 in 1997—many of them about California's past and the colorful characters who rode our trails to fame or infamy.

To date he has sold more than 180,000-plus copies of his first book, "Little Known Tales in California History", and has done respectably well with most of his other titles.

But until fate derailed his 33-year journalism career, he never aspired to write a book, and certainly never anticipated he would come to be regarded as "Mr. Self-Publishing" by his peers in the Sacramento area. "I would have liked living in the Old West," he says. "I wanted, at one time, to be a really good cowboy. I had horses as a young man and even took a raw colt and trained it to work cattle."

But, by the time Pryor was born on March 19, 1927, the era of gunslingers and gold miners was over, and he started life, instead, on his family's farm outside of King City in the Salinas Valley.

He was terminated after writing for 27 years for a magazine. The magazine was sold to a Midwest firm.

Pryor turned to writing books and says now, "I wish I had been fired 20 years earlier."

Index

www.ingramcontent.com/pod-product-compliance
Lightning Source LLC
LaVergne TN
LVHW051513080426
835509LV00017B/2049